Modern Mentality and Evangelization

By Charles Moeller

Translated by E. Mike-Bekassy

alba house
DIVISION OF THE SOCIETY OF ST. PAUL
STATEN ISLAND, N.Y. 10314

Part 3: JESUS & MARY

NIHIL OBSTAT
DONALD A. PANELLA, M.A., S.T.L., S.S.L.
Censor Librorum

IMPRIMATUR
✠ TERENCE C. J. COOKE, D.D.
New York, N. Y. — April 24, 1968

Library of Congress Catalog Card Number: 68-15380

PREFACE

THE system of ideas in this work is arranged along two main lines of thought, the one is contemporary mentality, its subject is religious sociology; the other is a doctrinal and catechetic orientation dealing with evangelism. The four themes: God, Christ, the Virgin Mary and the Church, are therefore considered from two aspects; one from the world to be saved, and the other from the heavenly Jerusalem, which is to appear one day, adorned like a bride come to meet her husband, Christ.

The sociological aspects can easily be deduced. Jean Guitton writes: "We have arrived at the pathetic moment when man, believing that he can know and do everything, suddenly realizes that the most he can do is to destroy himself. After that man will either remain in darkness or rise to the light. Belief in God will neither come from above, in the form of Revelation, nor from within man, pure reason, but will surge up from the tears of experience."

The doctrinal and catechetic orientation follows the biblical, patristic and liturgical revival. Mauriac writes: "We must rid ourselves of our packaged, ready-made ideas, rigid systems, and open out to that Love whose witnesses we are here on earth." Christianity is Jesus Christ. A superficial agreement between religious sociology and revelation should not be sought. It is from the depth of the abyss where man, who is against God and at the same time obsessed by Him, calls for help from biblical, ecclesial and liturgical catechetics. This providential answer to the evils of this world is the only possible one. It is to believe and hope in our Christian message; it is to love with the love Jesus gave us, the love of the Holy Spirit dwelling in us.

No new methods can be found here: no magical formula

or "short cuts." The call to Christ comes unrestrainably from where evil is concealed deepest. Bear witness to this and tell the world of it, and it will become apparent how the world of God and the world of men "are groping to find and to make contact with each other."

The description of the contemporary mind will be limited to two essential points. The only novelty is perhaps that we have endeavored to present a wider scope of religious problems by including the beliefs of our separated brothers. The object of the part on "ecumenism" is well expressed by a specialist on the subject: "This problem is difficult, since there is the risk of attributing to the Church a lack which should be attributed to her members. I am not prepared to admit that in any point of faith Lutherans or Anglicans have a more perfect doctrine than has the Catholic Church, who has the protection of Christ. But it is certain that there are Catholics who are less stirred by the gratuitousness of grace, by the holiness of the Bible, or the mystical beauties of the Church than they should be. Doubtless they could find admirable models within the Church in that which they themselves lack. However, it is possible that they might receive useful lessons outside the Church which they cannot find in their immediate surroundings. Thus it can be said that the return of our separated brothers would turn our attention toward the spiritual treasures of the Church which we are not sufficiently utilizing.[1]

It is not my intention to present doctrinal orientations and catechetic perspectives as a miniature theology, but only to trace an outline, by endeavoring to state the true position in the vast theological and catechetic revival.

Rather than to give a didactic exposition we have endeav-

---

1. Ch. Boyer, *Le probleme de la reunion des Chretiens* in *Unitas*, (French ed.) I. (1948) p. 14-15.

ored to trace, — through deduction and induction — a theological spirit and mind inspired by the Bible and Liturgy. The evangelization suggested in this work is but the spirit of the Church, her ordinary Magisterium incarnate in the liturgy and in the Bible as prayed and lived in Jesus, on whom it centers.

This book was intended to be concise and at the same time clear, its object is to consult the reader, rather than to be read. The large-type text deals with what is essential, while the small type brings technical specifications for a more advanced catechetics, or concrete examples to illustrate general statements. The bibliography has been reduced to a minimum, to make its use easy.

Thanks are due to the review *Lumen Vitae* and to its untiring director, Father G. Delcuve, to whom this work owes its existence. It is in fact made up of articles written for this magazine. The chapters on sociology, on the Church and the two doctrinal chapters on God and on Christ were specially written for this book. The whole has been revised as far as possible so as to form a summa for use in evangelism. We heartily thank the director of *Lumen Vitae* for his encouragement and suggestions.

If this essay could encourage and bring light to the heralds of faith; help one single soul to its salvation, it will not have been written in vain. The preacher, the catechist and the professor who will read this book should know that its author desires to be spiritually at their side in their search for the path leading to faith and its ecclesial testimony.

CONTENTS

PART I

JESUS

CHAPTER I

JESUS CHRIST IN THE
CONTEMPORARY MENTALITY

I. JESUS CHRIST FOR THE NON-CHRISTIANS

NEITHER the humanity of Jesus, nor his divinity, are correctly
understood in the non-Christian world. Either Jesus is considered
only a man, or else only a god, in either case his "incarnation"
has not the orthodox meaning Christianity gives it.

1. WHEN JESUS IS ONLY MAN

The Judeo-Christians regarded Jesus as the greatest prophet,
but refused to recognize him as the son of God.[1] After eighteen
centuries of history, Renan, in his "Life of Jesus" painted an
idyllical (and false) picture of one he called "a perfect man,"
"a gentle idealist," "a pacific revolutionary." There are a great
number of non-Christians who profess deep admiration for the
man Jesus. Without too great a risk of error one can distinguish
two trends: the first sees in Jesus an almost perfect incarnation

---

1. On Judeo-Christianism see H. J. Schoeps, *Theologie und Geschichte
des Juden-Christentum*, Tübingen, 1949, 526 pp. (Reviewed in *Hist. eccl.*
XLVII [1952] pp. 212-216).

of the religious sentiment; the second likes to see in him his love for the "humble and the offended." Jesus the man is made out to be the first prophet of a sort of "evangelical socialism."

Those non-Christians who see in Jesus a testimony of religious sentiment historically belong in the sphere of liberal Protestantism. In 1888, Harnack traced Christianity back to the revelation of filial sentiment towards God the Father. He said that this purely inner religion should be freed of its mythological ornaments (what the Catholics call dogma), and this purified Christian faith would be one of the simplest and most universal among religious sentiments: the sentiment of a dependency on God tinged with an expression of confidence in other great non-Christian religions, for example the Brahmanism of Ramanoudja. The central presupposition is that Jesus is not the incarnate *God.*

Another variation on the subject of Christ is represented by Gide, who is typical in this regard. In *Nourritures terrestres* he paints Jesus as nothing more than a prophet of joy (in the Gidean sense, a sort of pantheistic hedonism). The Gospel, he says, doesn't contain a single word on "renunciation or asceticism." The words "God is love" should be reversed and turned into "Love is God." Man's wonder and delight, ever ready for the novelty of sensation, is a kind of love of man towards the world. The necessary detachment for this sort of "evangelical Epicurianism" would be the true meaning of the message of Jesus. Christ was one of the witnesses to terrestrial joys, and to the progress of the world through man's virtue — virtue being the only divine thing on earth and identical with love (always in the Gidean sense). When the crucified Christ cried out in his abandon and his solitude, he was testifying that there was no personal God, no Heavenly Father, and *that he had been mistaken* when he invoked his Father. As Prometheus he had been punished on the cross for having loved mankind. The Evangelists have misled us by representing the "one who died *through* sinners" as having "died *for* sinners." As for the doctrine of renunciation, this originates from St. Paul (who is thus opposed to the Gospel), and the Church, which has thus distorted, for reasons of moral power, the true face of Jesus. All the dogmatic and moral apparatus of Christianity is nothing more than a myth suited to sustain the first efforts in the infancy of mankind. But once an adult age is reached, it should reject these early stages and face a reality in a way worthy of man. For man faces the blind world alone, just as Jesus had.[2]

The second trend which dominates the non-Christian world regarding Jesus derives from those "Christian truths gone crazy" of which Chesterton spoke. They are still widespread, for they are sustained by powerful social currents. Maurras' statement on the "revolutionary ferment of the *Beatitudes* and the *Magnificat*," is well known, and the Church ought to have purged Catholicism of them through its political and social organizations. Historically this trend of social evangelization can be traced to the 18th and 19th centuries. For a time it served as vehicle for some Christian ideas which lacked dogma — the famous "perfume of the broken vase," of which Renan spoke. Actually, there are a number of atheist revolutionaries who see in Jesus a distant formulator of socialism; sometimes, they say, they would willingly accept the Gospel, but they cannot but fight with all their force a Christianity the Church has so definitely compromised with the capitalist regime. Of course the Jesus of the Gospels, whom they admire, is in no way a god, only the incarnation of the religion of man, or rather of the religion of the people.

All categories of thought, which today represent these two trends in exegetics as well as in science and in philosophy, are of the past. Let us not be illuded. This rationalism which values in Jesus and his message "the perfume of a perfume, and soon

---

2. The reader can find more details on the above in *Littérature du XXme siècle et christianisme*, Vol. 1, Chap. on Gide.

the shadow of a shadow," has still a great many adherents. It is as important as ever to establish by *as rigorous methods as possible* that it is *reasonable* to believe in the divinity of Jesus.

2. Christ's Incarnation Is but One "Atavar" Among a Number of Others

There are non-Christians who see in Jesus only an incarnation of the divine, or the Absolute. This incarnation is nothing more than a manifestation among a number of others, the successive descents of God into time, for example such as Osiris, Vishnu, Zoroaster, the Buddha, etc. In other words Jesus is but one example (some say the most perfect) of the revelation of the transcendent God brought to man imprisoned in time and matter. Beyond apparent differences between these incarnations of the absolute, it is necessary to rise to a universal and identical religious substratum. This substratum is best expressed by the Hindu and Persian mystics. Those who see in Jesus only the man, make the error attributed to the Nestorian heresy; those, on the other hand, who only see in him a *transitory* epiphany of an impersonal absolute are, without knowing it, inspired by Docetic teaching and other types of Gnosticism. Religious relativism imperils the unique and transcendent character of Jesus.

Thomas Mann, though tending towards profane humanism (at least before the open crisis in *Doctor Faustus*), is an example of this "Alexandrian syncretism," in (*Joseph and his Brethren*). The present epoch, haunted by an apocalyptic tragedy, is easily attracted by any syncretistic philosophy. The literary critic of the London Times used the expression "Alexandrian syncretism" in regard to Huxley's *Perennial philosophy.* "The minimum explicative hypothesis" to which the author of "*Point Counterpoint*" reduces every religion, is a vague syncretism, predominantly Gnostic. It is also an inhuman synthesis, for it refuses to save time and matter. The idea of the "astronaut without any ballast" is absolutely un-Christian, since it rejects God's real and unique incarnation into time and space through the mediation of Jesus Christ. The same can be said of the "mystical" novels of Somerset Maugham, Charles Morgan and D'Abellio.

Religious relativism in its endless forms of Gnostic, Oriental mysticism and metaphychicism is an acute danger, because it is veiled by an apparently universal religious mysticism. Moreover, these ideologies are attractive because they promise a sensible contact between the faithful and the invisible. The figure of Jesus is drowned in a flood of distorted religious traditions, fitting into the general pattern of this syncretism.

Although Simone Weil in her life as in the greater part of her ideas cannot be subjected to this criticism, the central intuition in her religious thinking is Gnostic. She says in several places in her *Note-Books (Cahiers)* and repeats in *Lettre à un réligieux,* that there may have been several incarnations of Jesus. Moreover, a central statement in her thinking is the rejection of the Old Testament, and the value she attaches to Egyptian, Hindu, Persian and Greek religious traditions. In its essence, and despite great beauty in detail, Simone Weil's philosophy is a revival of Catharism. She only wants to see the passion of Jesus. She denies the resurrection of the Savior's humanity. Such a doctrine cannot any longer be "partially Christian" for it is not Christian at all, Christianity is *in Jesus.* The incarnate God *is* resurrected, and gives meaning to death *and* of life. The infatuation of too many Christians for the ideas of Simone Weil is a typical sign of the religious relativism that marks the religious trend of our century. Gnosis is a standing temptation to the spirit which has not understood (or has disregarded) Christ. This is the temptation *par excellence,* which forever turns its back on Jesus (obviously only heretical Gnosis is meant).[3]

---

3. See *Cahiers sioniens,* June 1952, *Simone Weil devant l'église et l'Ancien Testament.*

Religious relativism is wide-spread. Actually those categories of methods of research upon which its arguments are based are surpassed in exegetics as well as in the history of religion, philosophy and theology. Unfortunately an easy play of comparatives between Jesus and for example Buddha will always appeal to the wide public which has naturally no idea of differences in the complex discipline of the history of religion. Not everybody can know that experts no longer consider the system of Reizenstein as valid. It is only the serious researcher who is aware of the absence of historical specifications which mark these approaches. The atmosphere of catastrophe in which we live invites hypothetic explanations; they turn Jesus into an Atavar of the Absolute. Therefore, it is necessary to explain to the student of apologetics the real state of affairs in religious studies. *Christus* by Huby remains an indispensable book, although out-dated on many points.

II. JESUS CHRIST FOR NON-CATHOLIC CHRISTIANS

It is difficult to find the right balance between two poles of inconsistency whose link remains a mystery. We have condemned the Nestorian and the Monophysitic heresies, but beyond these there are many imponderables. Besides real heresy, warpings or exclusivism must always be feared. A slight error on central points leads to infinite deviations. The true Christ must be presented

---

4. The basic book on the Council of Chalcedon, the essential "Christologic" Council is *Chalkedon, Geschichte und Gegenwart*, Würtzburg, Echter, 1951-1954, published under the direction of A. Grillmeier and H. Bacht of the Faculty of the S. J. of Frankfurt. The first volume contains a series of historical and doctrinal essays on the pre-history and the history of the Council. Vols. II and III deal with the history of the Council up to our days. Read the review in Rev. l'Hist. eccl. XLVIII (1953) p. 252-261; XLIX (1954) p. 896-907; XL (1955) p. 916-919. More easily accessible is Y. Congar, *Tradition and Traditions in the Church,*

and taught.[4] Even if all of the many heresies are avoided, the risk of leaving in the shadow one or another aspect of the person of Christ can have incalculable consequences. The disunity of Christian Churches is a tragic proof.[5]

1. JESUS CHRIST IN ORTHODOXY

Without entering into further detail, it can be said that Oriental anthropology is centered around the idea of *Transfiguration;* man is truly himself when identified with what he truly is, that is to say the image of God. He becomes deified.

Not to see the wonderful humanism saturating Byzantine liturgy is completely to misunderstand it. But while we in the West have a tendency *to oppose* the majestic aspect of God the Father with the human aspect of God the Son, there is perhaps nothing more characteristic of Byzantine liturgy than the union between these two aspects. Doubtless this comes from the vitality of the theme of the divine picture in the East; a theme deteriorated into abstractions in the West. Since man himself is seen as a reflection of God, as a divine spark, *without which he would no longer be what he is,* there is union instead of opposition. To see Christ fully as a man in this perspective is not so much the antithesis of his divinity but its result.[6]

New York, 1966. For further research all necessary data can be found here. Also, the classical book of E. Masure, *Le sacrifice du chef,* Paris, a number of editions, finally our own articles on the Council in *Collectanea mechliniensia,* 1951, Nos. 2 and 4; 1952, No. 3 in *Questions liturgiques et parossiales,* 1952, No. 1 (on Chalcedon and the liturgy) in *La Vie Intellectuelle,* December 1951 (history of the Council, outlines its importance).

5. The roots of the schism perhaps do not lie in Mariology or Ecclesiology, but in Christology (this again is dominated by anthropology and the doctrine on justification, the three elements being inextricably mixed).

6. L. Bouyer, *Les catholiques et la liturgie byzantine, Dieu Vivant,* 1952, No. 21, p. 27.

In Oriental spirituality and liturgy, Christ's humanity appears above all divinized and transfigured (note for example the importance of the Feast of the Transfiguration in the East). Byzantine liturgy is a sort of anticipation of the heavenly Jerusalem. Byzantine art, too, is a visible means, a window open on the invisible world. The liturgy of the Byzantine Holy Week puts the real sufferings of Jesus into a form wherein the glorious Alleluiah of the celestial city constantly recurs (in the West the Alleluiah is omitted in Lent). In the same way the prayer to the incarnate *Logos* is frequent, while the Latin liturgy prefers "through Jesus Christ, our Lord" (but the East, too, of course has kept this form). It is enough to see and hear the holy liturgy unfold in order to enter, in ways, into contact with the glorified humanity of the Savior

Seen from this point, the suffering of Jesus becomes "passion of God" (according to the flesh, the theologian adds). Byzantine spirituality solves the paradox of joining a keen sense of the sorrows with a vision of a divine glory shining through them.

In Dostoevski's works, characters like Myshkin, Aliusha, Dimitri Karamazov are incarnations of transfigured suffering. In *"The Twenty-Fifth Hour,"* Gheorghiu shows how batches of deportees form a sort of icon of the Christ, of the suffering *God.* We also point out, however, without stressing a deep tendency in Orthodoxy, above all in Hesychasm, which sees in the abandon of Jesus on the Cross a sort of mysterious *passion of divinity* itself. This idea has nothing to do with the theory of *Kenosis.*

If we pursue this line of thought we come to the famous "humility" of the Byzantine spirit; Christ, incarnate God, man transfigured, the *Logos* glorious in loneliness and suffering, is at the same time "merciful and a friend of man." In face of this glory the sinner prostrates himself with a heart-rending feeling of his total abandon and absolute confidence in his pardon.

It is here a case of the *Oumiliénié* (total humility) of the Orthodox spirit. Examples of it can be found in Dostoevski (Fiodor

Karamazov, Lebedev, Sonia, Marmaladov, etc.) and in the
"Tales of a Russian Pilgrim." The gesture of the monk Zossima,
as he prostrates himself before Dimitri Karamazov at the beginning
of the tale, is pure *oumiliénié.* It is because Godol was completely lacking in this sentiment, that he was finally devoured
by his fear of Satan, and destroyed the second half of *"Dead
Souls."* There is something of the *oumiliénié* in Tolstoi's "Idiots"
in *War and Peace.*

The vision of Christ in Eastern Christianity showing him
divine, human, suffering and merciful, but above all *transfigured,*
involves a number of consequences. We will point out two which
are only apparently contradictory: a certain disdain of all that
is temporal and historical (therefore humanistic progress) and
at the same time a sharp sense of the "cosmic" character of
Redemption, wherein the material universe, too, is transfigured.
It is sufficient to read what Zossima says in the *Brothers Karamazov* to see to what extent the Orthodox Church embraced the
revelation about the creation of the world according to the image
of the divine Word.

All these aspects of Jesus are true; although they above all
stress the divinity in our Lord, they constitute none the less
central truths on faith. The Christ of Orthodoxy is above all the
Christ of Easter; this Christology, not to mention St. Paul, is
chiefly inspired by St. John. In the eyes of the East, Roman
Catholicism yields to a temptation of a certain Nestorianism.

"Oriental tradition never made a clear distinction between
mysticism and theology, between the personal experience of divine
mysteries, and the dogma the Church affirms.... Dogma expressing a revealed truth which to us seems like an unfathomable
mystery, must be lived by us through a process in the course of
which, instead of assimilating the mystery to the way we understand it, we should look out for a profound change, an interior
transformation of our spirit in order to prepare it for mystical
experience. Far from being contradictory, theology and mysticism

justify and complete each other. The one is not possible without the other: while mystical experience is a personal enhancement of the contents of common faith, theology is an expression of what can be experienced by each for the good of all." [7]

This gulf between the absolute and the relative, between the Incarnate and the creatures, appears everywhere in the Old Testament and in Christian spiritual and theological matter. It is expressed in doctrines of "transcendency" and in the unknowableness of the divine essence. Created beings can know each other, but when they turn to God, they feel as if they are crushed under the weight of their total dependency, and in fact by their inexistence. Their only resource is to say that God *is not* what they can know of him, that he cannot be assimilated by any creature, any image, nor can any word express his being. Though unknown in his essence God has nevertheless revealed himself as Father, Son and Holy Spirit; the Son becomes man and the Holy Spirit descended upon the Church. The Christian God is not the "unknown God" who was venerated by the philosophers, but a living God who reveals himself and acts. This is the meaning of the Orthodox doctrine on the *energies* or divine actions, distinct from the unknowable essence, as formulated by St. Gregory Palamas in the 14th century. The Old Testament relates the divine acts which continue in the history of the chosen people, but Christian revelation leads us to a fulfillment: the Son of God "dispossessed himself, and took the nature of a slave, fashioned in the likeness of man, and presented himself to us in human form. Then he lowered his own dignity by accepting the obedience which brought him to death, death on a cross" (Phil. 2, 7-8, quoted from the Knox translation). Hereafter the divine acts do not reach man from the exterior only, but their very source is in human nature, divinized by Jesus Christ. Henceforth, it is no longer a case of merely

---

7. V. Lossky, *Essai sur la théologia mystique de l'Église d'Orient*, Paris, 1944, pp. 6-7.

recognizing the transcendency and the omnipotence of God, but also of accepting the salvation he grants us and assimilating the divine life he has given us. This is what the Fathers called "deification"; God has become man so that we may become God. This deification is accomplished by our aggregation to the body of Christ and the unction of the Holy Spirit on each one of us as a person. The economy of the Holy Spirit consists precisely in making us all communicate throughout the centuries of history, between the Ascension and the Parousia, into one single humanity deified by Jesus Christ: "God has sent into our hearts the Spirit of the Son who calls Abba, Father!" (Gal. 4, 6).[8]

To sum up this introduction to Orthodox Christology is a passage from Palamas: "Since the Son of God, in his inconceivable love for man, has not only joined his divine hypostasis to our nature, and having taken a body with a soul, and a soul having intelligence, appeared on earth and lived among men, and even, O magnificent miracle, united with human hypostases themselves, and by fusing with every one of the faithful through the communion of his Holy Body, became concorporal with us and made of us a temple of the entire divinity, for the plenitude of divinity lives corporally in him (Col. 2, 9). Would he not illuminate, by encompassing them in the light of the divine brilliance of his body which is in us, the souls of them who participate worthily, as he illuminated the bodies of his disciples on Mount Tabor? Then indeed that body possessing the course of the light of grace was not yet confounded in our bodies; it lighted up from the exterior those who approached worthily and allowed the light to penetrate into their souls through their sensible eyes. But today he is mingled with us, he lives within us, and naturally he illuminates our soul from within. Only One, Christ, can see

---

8. J. Meyendorf, *L'Église Orthodoxe, Hier et aujourd'hui* (Coll. Les Univers), Paris, 1960, pp. 164-5.

God. We must be united with Christ in an intimate union to see God." [9]

2. CHRIST IN ANGLICANISM

It is not easy to speak of "Christ in Anglicanism" since "there is no specifically Anglican theological doctrine. The Church of England teaches the doctrines of the Catholic faith, found in Holy Scripture; in the Apostles' Creed (in the Nicene and the Athanasian Creeds) and in the decisions of the first four general Councils of the undivided Church."

The following is by an Anglican theologian, Bishop Stephen Neill: "Let anyone show us anything clearly expressed in Holy Scripture that we do not teach, and we will teach it. Let him point out anything in our teaching or in our practice clearly contrary to Holy Scripture, and we will abandon it." In the matter of theological interpretation, and in individual belief the Anglican Churches permit greater freedom than do some others. But the faith of the Church is contained in the Bible and in the Prayer Book, and the Anglican Churches have never agreed to compromise on this faith.

These ideas remind the author of a brief description of the various aspects of Anglican life. By it, though there is no "Anglican faith, there is an Anglican attitude and an Anglican atmosphere." Therein you will find a "biblical quality which gives the precise limits and directions of Anglican life. At every moment theology refers to Scripture." These churches are "liturgical." "There is a sober and moderate style of devotion which characterizes our Churches the world over. The aim is not to obtain immediate sentimental effects, but progressively to construct a determined and resolute will for sanctity, based rather on the education of

---

9. Quoted by J. Meyendorf and reproduced in C. Moeller, G. Philips *Grace et oecumenisme* (Coll. *Irénikon*), Chevetogne, 1957, p. 57.

the will than on stimulating sentiment." Another mark of "the true Anglican is his intense sense of continuity," expressed among other things "in the importance Anglicanism attaches to the episcopate and episcopal ministry." This respect for the past perhaps explains the "Anglican tradition of theological sciences. Anglicanism always turned to Scripture, to the Church Fathers and to history." Elsewhere, "it is because they have such great confidence in truth that the Anglican Churches demand so much of their faithful. . . . To be a good Anglican is an extremely exacting enterprise and it remains exacting through life. The Anglican Churches treat their faithful not like children who must be kept on the lead under all sorts of rules, but like adult Christians who must learn to choose and decide as if they were before God and helped by the Holy Spirit who had been promised them." Finally regarding the famous *Comprehensiveness* our author says: "from the outset the Anglican Church made an effort to be comprehensive. Its end was to unite into one single body all whom God has united as one nation. . . . Perhaps these tensions should not be regarded as weaknesses, but as the price to pay for the privilege of a particular vocation." [10]

Among Christian confessions the Anglican Church forms a kind of bridge; it is important in teaching religion to stress the fact that Anglicanism is not Protestantism. In a way it is a link between Eastern Byzantinism and the Latin West. Anglicanism has a sharp sense of Christ's humanity and a no-less bright vision of his glorious divinity. It still maintains contact with the tradition of the Fathers, above all the Greeks (*Irenaeus* in the first place); and this explains the richness of Anglican Christology. From the Greek Fathers, Anglicanism takes the sense of Jesus' transfigured humanity, and this is the reason why Anglicanism has a double

---

10. S. Neill, *Anglicanism*, Baltimore.

richness: it has always kept deep concern for liturgical rites and insisted on the cosmic character of redemption.

The curious doctrine of *Kenosis* should also be mentioned. It tempted a certain number of Anglican theologians: a distinction should be drawn between the "Liberal Christianity of the Low Church," and the "non-Roman Catholic" Christianism of the High Church, and the Anglo-Catholicism of a very small minority. But the closer Anglicanism remains to the original ideas of its first theologians, the more it finds the way to a rich and complex Christology. What has saved Anglicanism is that it has been spared, at least at the beginning, the influence of Protestant doctrines on justification and predestination. In proportion as it is detaching itself from Calvinism which at one time had put its mark on it, Anglicanism is orienting in a direction which draws it closer to Orthodoxy and Catholicism.

All this may seem strange to one who is not acquainted with the *Pietas anglicana,* the sobriety, the somewhat rigid grandeur together with a latent tenderness in the way Psalms are sung. It is above all therein that the face of the traditional Anglican Christ appears, sovereign, yet near, participating in the majesty of God and the same time sensible to the soul, in that English imagination where the spiritual meets the sensible. "Our Lord and Savior": Whoever has heard these two words, spoken or sung, is aware that they contain grandeur and intimate proximity, both so characteristic of Anglican piety.

"You are seeking a philosophical religion, Sir," said William Law to John Wesley one day, "but that does not exist. Religion is the simplest thing in the world: we love God because he loved us first." The metaphysical English poets, such as Traherne or George Herbert, possess an extraordinary sense for the metaphysical diffused in the sensible world, and also a divination of the presence of the Savior in the world, in the Church and in the heart of each of the faithful. The proximity of the person Jesus, loved with secret tenderness, never obscures the majesty of the Savior. There is continuity from the universal Lord of the world who penetrates everything by his transfiguring holiness, to him to whom devotion has always been kept up by the Caroline divines, to the Savior who kindled fire in souls, a fire which burned in the heart of John Wesley.

Contemporary Evangelicalism has approached certain traditions of the "non-Roman Catholicism," through the influence of the biblical revival. It is becoming the forward wing of Anglicanism. The younger elements of the High Church also approach Evangelicalism. A liturgical, sacramental and parochial revival marks this branch even in industrial parishes. Both "Evangelical Catholicism" and "Catholic Evangelism" are awakening to the deep meaning of Anglicanism.

What is immediately striking in the Prayer Book is its markedly biblical stamp. The invocations of the litanies link the psalm prayer with the praying Church. Readings from the Bible and from the Old and New Testaments insert Church prayers between hearings of the Word of God. The kind of luminous and at the same time etherial joy expressed in the Hymns wherein the piety of all is for all, and yet addressed to each separately, so that every person remains in his own privacy which is never aloofness, sums up this picture of Anglican piety. The Communion Service is more clearly marked by firm but gentle petition and joy (which never attains the height of the *jubilus* of Gregorian Chant) and listening to the Gospel. When the liturgy of the Gospel is over, the community participating at the service of the Lord gathers around the altar. The eucharistic praise is entirely marked by the idea of hidden mystery, communicated in faith. Christ is he who gathers all together, calling each by his name, but in view of the Kingdom.[11]

---

11. M. Villain, *Introduction to oecumenism* (Coll. *église vivante*), 3rd Ed., Tournai, Paris, 1961, pp. 110-118.

On the purely musical plane Handel's *Messiah* perfectly expresses this mixture of majesty and grandeur which is sometimes solemn and slightly archaic, personal, and has ecstatic tenderness, the union of all of which is the priceless treasure of *Pietas Anglicana*.

3. The Christ of The Reformation

At the time of the liberal Protestantism, the Reformation suffered a grave crisis in dogma. By the end of the 19th century, the majority of the Protestant theologians and exegetes no longer believed in Christ's divinity. Certainly the pastors who taught religion to Gide did not, hence the dogmatic weakness which from the outset marks Gidean "Christianity."

Happily things have changed since. Leading Protestants are reverting to the firm belief in the divinity of Jesus, man and God. The Protestant Reformation affirms its adherence to the formula of the Council of Chalcedon. This return to a true faith in Jesus Christ can also explain the patristic and liturgical revival which now marks a great part of Protestantism.

However, a twofold danger threatens Christology. It is apparently contradictory, and is contained in the fundamental attitude of the doctrine of justification. We know the doctrine of the Reformation on the subject of justification: God's intervention in salvation presented as an occasional contact, like a tangent touching the circle only at one single point. There is no real incarnation of the divine into the human. Doubtless this idea throws light on one truth which is sometimes rather overlooked in the Catholicism of some of the faithful, namely the absolute transcendence of God, who is the only Savior and the only Redeemer. But this "theological occasionalism" is reflected in their Christology and is thereby threatened with Nestorianism and Monophysitism.

By its insistence on God as the only Savior, the Reformation was brought to stress above all "the Redeemer God" in Jesus

Christ; some of Luther's and Calvin's texts [12] give the impression that in the work of justification (not work of *"sanctification,"* nor of "second justification") the part of Jesus' humanity is obliterated: at times it gives the impression of being superfluous.

Elsewhere, throwing a strong light on the humiliation of Jesus' humanity, the Reformation likes to develop what it calls *theologia Crucis,* as opposed to *theologia Gloriae,* which it likes to attribute to Catholics. It interprets in the literal sense what St. Paul said of Jesus "that he became sin for our sake" and that "he accepted to be shamed on the wood of the cross." The Reformation defies the doctrines of divinization of human nature, in Christ, as in the faithful. In its view Christ's resurrection is above all an eschatological event; it is in an obscure faith, in the total submission of the soul to the Savior, in a submissive waiting for a "salvation beyond time" that the faithful are saved.

"Monophysitism," in insisting on a God-Savior, "Nestorianism" in its predilection for the *theologia Crucis,* are the two joint perils of reformed Christology. The Christ of the Reformation, while profoundly human (in the sense of the humiliated condition of sinner assumed) and fully divine, sole Savior like God, present in a clear light certain essential aspects of Christian truths. He has that sombre and prophetic grandeur in which, following Luther, Kierkegaard and Barth clothed the figure of the Savior. Here again it is not so much because it affirms, but because it denies, that the Reformation runs the risk of distorting the figure of Jesus.

The inner life of Protestantism could teach us much more than abstract polemics. A text by A. Monod can give some idea of the inner nature of Reformed piety. "If among the crosses you are given to carry there is one which seems to you, I do not say

---

12. In Y. Congar *op. cit.,* pp. 32-38 and *Chalkedon,* Vol. III, p. 459 sv. and 505 sv.

heavier to bear than the others, but one endangering your ministry, one that may forever ruin every hope of your holy mission, wherein from outside temptation joins with temptation from within, whereby your body, your spirit, and your very heart are hit, so that they seem forever lost, well, then I would say accept this cross, this assemblage of many crosses, with a particular feeling of submission, hope and gratitude, as if it were some infirmity through which the Lord has made you find a new mission. Hail it as the point of departure of a ministry of bitterness and weakness reserved by God for the end as the best, in which he will make more abundant the fruits of life than ever in your strong and joyous ministry they could have ever been in the past." [13]

J. S. Bach gives a good example of the Lutheran's ardent and gentle feeling for Jesus. The song *Mein Jesu Gute Nacht,* evokes the peace which descends on the world after the great uproar of the Passion. It has a tender note of familiarity, as if the faithful took into their custody the humanity of Jesus crucified by their own sins; the same time the evocation of universal peace which follows invokes the image of the dove returning to the Ark at dusk, and prolongs the fervor for the salvation which God alone can give. The desire to die in order to join Jesus is also expressed in the hymn *Komm, O süsse Tod;* there is little that could better interpret the kind of mistrust the Reformation has for, what it interprets as, excesses of a theology of a glory, too triumphant and too human in its accents. Doubtless we jump too readily from the Jesus, the man, dead and in peace in his grave in Jerusalem, to the triumphant God, without heeding that between the first stage and the second it is this *humanity* which suffers and is revived.

It is well to point out that in Lutheran doctrine the sense of the Eucharist has remained closer to Catholic truth; in it the

---

13. Quoted by M. Villain, *Introduction a l'Oecumenisme* (Coll. Église vivante) 3rd Ed. Tournai-Paris, 1961, p. 92.

humanity of the Lord is present with an evidently dynamical presence, but nevertheless real. At its limit this affirmation of divine action of this humanity is carried so far that it leads to ubiquity which tends to attribute to the humanity glorified by Jesus qualities which belong to the incommunicable divinity. On the other hand in Calvinism it seems that after the Resurrection the humanity of Jesus appears no more. The famous *Extra Calvinisticum* seems to insinuate that after ascending to heaven *remoto velamine humanitatis* the Lord God is directly revealed to the elect. It seems that sanctification is then worked directly by God, or, what is the same thing, by the Holy Spirit, without passing through the humanity of the Savior. We can see that in the swing from a "Nestorian" exaggeration of the life of Jesus on earth, to a "Monophysitism" in which, after the Resurrection and the Ascension, the human is too much absorbed by the divine, there is a difference in shade as represented by Calvinism or Lutheranism. Needless to say that movements of rejuvenation, such as Neo-Calvinism, of which we will speak later, are about to do away with these tendencies, which should not be interpreted literally.

III. JESUS CHRIST IN THE FAITH OF THE CATHOLICS

What Watkin calls the *Catholic center* appears clearly in the ordinary and the extraordinary Magisterium of the Church. The Latin liturgy and the Ecumenical Councils could reveal them if better known and made more use of in teaching about Christ. There is astonishing balance in Jesus between the human and the divine. St. Thomas' Christology agrees with the Council of Chalcedon; by the idea of created grace, it puts in the center of all theology the vision of the *humanity* of Jesus as the united instrument of salvation. We also know that, in spite of the privileged

place of the Angelic Doctor in systematic Catholic theology, the
Church has always allowed wide scope to other theological schools;
the Christology of Bonaventure and Duns Scotus, which are now
being more closely studied, can add important nuances to the
view of the supernatural life of the Savior's humanity; [14] although
this is a delicate problem, it is probable that modern discoveries
in psychology will give us a better understanding of the Savior's
life.[15]

Is this fundamental equilibrium of Catholic Christology reflected in ordinary teaching of theologians, in pastoral sermons
or in current spirituality? We fear that much is lacking; there is
always the danger of "Nestorianism" and "Monophysitism."

1. THE NESTORIAN DANGER

Catholics are often too human in their moral conceptions: when
they devote themselves to social Christianity they tend to see
in Christ only the militant leader, a companion. In the same way,
when trying to paint the human face of the Savior, they indulge
in undue intimacies which are not only in bad taste, but can
lead to theological errors. To concretize the figure of Jesus does
not mean to deprive it of its majesty. There is a painful and
sentimental spirituality which in our eyes lowers the figure of
the Savior, an example of this is the jaded and insipid iconography
attributed to St. Suplice. In a word, Catholic piety is very often
seriously lacking in religious virtue; it forgets reverential awe,

---

14. The tenets of Franciscan theology can play a part in enhancing
the humanity of Christ. That there is a "monophysite" danger in certain
Thomistic theologians is convincingly shown by P. Galtier, *La conscience
humain du Christ. A propos de quelques publications récentes,* in Gregor-
ianum, XXXII, 1951, pp. 526-568.

15. P. Galtier, *L'unité du Christ, Etre, Personne, Conscience,* Paris,
1939, XX - 378 pp. is still the fundamental work in this subject.

the awe of God in the Old Testament, or the awe which filled the disciples at the sight of the resurrected Savior.

The revision of religious language, which can easily become solemn and even pompous, is permissible, but within limits. Bible translations which give (Monsieur in French) "Sir" for "*Kurios*," and "Madam" for "*Despoina*" make one feel uneasy. And what are we to think of books which call Jesus, the Lord of Heaven, the "man of the hut," "good boy," and "fine fellow," "good chap"? We must also point out a literature, pious only in name, where the Sacred Heart is spoken of in terms of "prisoner of the tabernacle who suffers from the abandon of man." This is simply to forget that in the Eucharist the *resurrected* Christ is present. If we want to revive devotion to the Sacred Heart it must be absolutely freed of absurd terms which bring the glory of Jesus down to the level of a human, a far-too human, friend. We should also insist on pointing out how much of the Christmas piety is marred; how often the faithful never go beyond a pious sentimentality of the Crib. A friend once made the witty remark: "These Nestorian Cribs are all the faith most Catholics have." This may be an exaggeration, but the danger is there. St. Bernard was saddled (on the evidence of a series of authentic and interpolated texts) with a very sentimental cult of Jesus' humanity.[16] What can one say of Stations of the Cross, which nowhere reflect the truth that the one who is being crucified is a God-man. It is a pity that the traditional arrangement of the Stations (the Church prescribes 14 Stations without specifying their subject) all stop at the putting into the grave, and do not continue to the resurrection where the divinity is manifested. The office of Good Friday, too, is misunderstood.

It is also a pity that manifestations are limited to the Way

---

16. *Saint Bernard Théologien*, Acts of the Congress of Dijon, September 15-19, 1953, (Coll. *Anal* S.O. List XI, [1953], 2nd. Vol.) Rome.

of the Cross without a ceremony on Holy Saturday in honor of the Resurrection.

In social Christianity there is the danger of only seeing the man Christ, the fighting man, the cornerstone of a social edifice that is purely human. It cannot be repeated too often that the sense of God is lacking in modern man, even when he is a Christian; a clear proof of this is the faint "Nestorian" hint in some modern Christian literature.

2. THE "MONOPHYSITIC" DANGER

Though Catholics are sometimes "Nestorian" in their moral and spiritual life, they are also often "Monophysitic" in their theology and their sacramental spirituality. Very often pious souls see in Jesus Christ the "Good God." It was God alone who in Jesus Christ bent down to man "in various borrowed forms" as Canon Masure puts it in characterizing this deviation.

Here are some examples to demonstrate this point. In the minds of many of the faithful, whether consciously or not, it is God who acts directly (*formaliter*, as the theologian says) in Jesus. In Christ it is God who *does everything*. In a recent enquiry in a high school it turned out that the majority of students thought that Christ had no human soul, and that in its place was the Word.[17] The same deviation with regard to the Eucharist, will lead to only seeing the presence of God; there is a way, of speaking glibly of "God in the Eucharist"; in commenting on the Mass it is said that at consecration God descends on the altar, thereby

---

17. Y. Congar, *op. cit.* p. 56. The following experiment can be recommended to all preachers and professors: to the question "Had Jesus a soul?" a good half will answer in the negative. This fact has something to make one feel anxious, if we think of the centuries of struggle of the Church, especially through the voice of the Patriarchs of Antioch, Theodore, and Theodoret to save this essential value. But all this hardly interests the faithful. Cf. III pp. 302-327.

forgetting that what is present in the sacrament is the body and
the blood of Jesus in his *Glorified Humanity.* (Obviously ontologically united with the Word.) In the same way the link between the sacrament of the Eucharist with the resurrection and
the incorporation of our whole being, soul *and body,* is no longer
perceived. There is so little understanding of the essential contact
between the Eucharist, body and blood of Jesus, and the sanctification of the material world, its transfiguration at the end of
all time. The perfect harmony between the ritual and sacramental
rites and the Eucharist, that is to say the glorious humanity of
Christ is no longer apparent. Here is the source of the disincarnate
deism which weakens Catholic piety.

Before summing up we should like to point out that Claudel
and Péguy are the two writers who can best help the teacher
of religion. Claudel started out from the will to "possess the
world" inspired by Romanticism. One of his earliest characters,
Tête d'or, says, "Like a tree I have need of deep roots and an
immense sky in order to stand upright." Death revealed to this
man who wanted "the perfect apple, that is the world," that the
only "tree" capable of giving him the depth of the earth and the
vastness of the sky is the *tree of the Cross.* Claudean characters,
Violaine, Rodrigue and Colombus, discover in the total despoil-
ment of suffering and death the powerful joy of the man who is
restored to his place as a king of Creation. In the death and the
resurrection of Jesus Christ Claudel's heroes recognize the union
with the suffering humanity of Jesus, and his exaltation to the
right hand of the Father. They also recognize the mystical nuptials
of the transfigured Adam with the regenerated universe. *Les cin-
ques grandes odes* (*The Five Great Odes*) are a lyrical outburst
of this Christian vision of the world.

Péguy was obsessed by the problem of evil, which he saw
most of all in the metaphysical aging of the created world. When
God, "young as well as eternal," became "internal" the temporal
through incarnation, even creation, filled with the youth of God,

instead of aging, is renewed ceaselessly, returning to the dawn, to that moment of the "Spring of grace and the Spring of nature" which Eve had known before the Fall. Péguy's central idea of time "temporally eternal," partly inspired by Bergson, also springs from a profound vision of the doctrine of the catechism. The incarnation of the eternal into the temporal, of which Péguy continually speaks, is extended into the Church and the sacraments: Jesus is there, "as on the first days." The "temporally eternal" is at the root of Péguy's admirable Christian *realism*. It gives birth to the famous saying: "for the supernatural is itself carnal." This is no mere oratory, but the expression in superbly simple, primitive and robust language of one of the central Christian truths, namely the incarnation of the Word, God-man, time and space through the sacraments and the Church.

The figure of Jesus as portrayed in Malègue's works, the half-light of faith alternately hiding and revealing God, is the "shining cloud" of the incarnation of the Word; God accepting to play the game of secondary causes, assuming the risks of being mixed up in just any human determinism, showing the sense of "the human holiness of the Savior."

In Mauriac the face of divine love can be seen: He sets out "into the desert of love" and to the "core of sin" in search for the sinner. This divine love is evidently the love of Jesus: this point though not always clear in his novels becomes clear in *Vie de Jésus*. Bernanos presents Jesus under the aspect of agony and joy. It is not possible to forget the figure of Jesus presented in the works of Sigrid Undset: mercy, love which calls, communion of all the saints in Jesus, judgment of the world, transfiguration of the planet.

CONCLUSION

Millions of people do not know Jesus Christ. Though God haunts the contemporary mind there are few who have discovered that the transcendent person to whom man either gives himself or whom he withstands is Jesus, suffering and resurrected. Christ is not spoken of, only socialism, happiness or progress. Everyone speaks about social Christianity, about a divine force guiding the world; but there is *only a small number of men who know Jesus Christ.*

Moreover, even those who speak about Jesus Christ do not always know him. Either they turn him into a pure man, (and what man can completely know another man?) or else they regard the unique incarnation as an Atavar of the Absolute, and in that case they let the visible world sink into a void for the sake of the impersonal ocean of the absolute.

Christians themselves do not always know Jesus in all his human and divine dimensions. This knowledge includes a clear comprehension of the tragedy of Christian disunity, it also includes some essential decisions in Christian life.[18]

---

18. In the *mentality of non-Christians* there is no notable change. The critics keep identifying Christianity with theology and say it is no longer valid. The person of Jesus is seldom mentioned. Camus is a notable exception for he confesses that he is conscious of the sacred, of the mystery there is in man: "I do not see why I should not acknowledge the emotion I feel for Christ and his teaching.... I have but respect and veneration for the person of Christ and his story, but I do not believe in His resurrection." This text of Camus, written in 1957, places the problem in its proper context: the resurrection is the most marked sign of the divinity of Jesus, it is the "theological" foundation of our salvation. Unable to believe in his resurrection, Camus and with him those who know Jesus, only see in him a human figure, whose greatness they do,

as a matter of fact, acknowledge. In *La chute*, Clamence expresses his emotion before the human being who slept on the ground for others, who, though innocent, refused to be innocent, and died in a way that obliterated everything so as not to be spared; he is the antithesis of Clamence himself, who tries to dilute his culpability in the deluge of a general culpability; Christ could not have borne the idea of the innocents Herod massacred on his account. Therein is a picture of the love Camus meant. (Note of 1962).

CHAPTER II

BIBLICAL ORIENTATIONS AND CATECHETIC PERSPECTIVES

SINCE this is a vast subject, it will be necessary to limit ourselves to essentials, namely *biblical material,* the main lines of *Council tradition and theology,* and *concrete suggestions.*

I. BIBLICAL MATERIAL

1. THE ANCIENT LAW

The Old Testament follows the lines of the twofold revelation; of God and of his Messiah. It is important to find the point at which the Incarnation joins the monotheistic revelation. After that the main outlines of Messianism can be drawn.

1. The "creative and revealing word" has already been mentioned in the first volume of my work. So has the Old Testament theme of the *presence* of God amongst his people. The images of the pillar of fire, the tabernacle of witness, the Glory of Yahweh resting on the Cherubim above the Ark of the Covenant are signposts leading to the Incarnation of the Son of God. St. John's "and the Word was made flesh and dwelt among us" proves it.

From the beginning the Incarnation is present in the history of salvation, that is to say in the presence of God amongst his people. "You shall be my people and I will be your God" — and by his extraordinary acts the Lord of Glory gradually builds up his Kingdom. The revelation of the project of salvation (therefore the preparation for the Incarnation) becomes more profound as it progresses parallel with God's manifestation as eternal, universal and within man. The coming of the Son of God is the summit of the project of salvation: it is the final, creative and redeeming "Word."

2. Messianism centers around three ideas: *Son of David, Son of Man,* and *Servant of Yahweh.* The expression Son of David sums up the descendance of the Messiah in the flesh, the temporal cradle whence he issued in Bethlehem, the city of David; the Virgin Mary herself was of the family of David. Around this first expression we shall explain all that pertains to the human nature of Jesus, perfectly consubstantial with our own nature while it is (and because it is) of the line of Abraham, the ancestor of the people of Israel. The expression *Son of Man,* contrary to a still too popular belief, does not in the first place signify the humanity of Jesus, but his *divine origin;* through Daniel it is in fact attached to the apocalyptical genre wherein appears a celestial being hidden in God, and even sometimes God himself, who will reveal himself "on the day of Yahweh" and will judge the world. Finally *Servant of Yahweh* calls attention to the suffering and redemptive character of the Messiah according to the texts of Isaias. It is only in the person of Jesus that all three aspects of the Messiah will manifest a mysterious unity.

Another series of texts stress that the Anointed of Yahweh will be King, Priest and *Prophet.* He will be Prophet because he will speak in the name of God and bear witness to the divine plan concerning the chosen people. He will be *King,* because, as a new David, he will reign in peace over his Kingdom; and at the same time with the breath of his mouth, he will annihilate the wicked, and render justice in the name of God. He will be *Priest*, because he will sanctify his people and will offer himself up like a lamb that is led to slaughter.

Finally, we must remember that the coming of the Messiah will be both *glorious* and *hidden;* it will be accompanied by striking miracles, especially in the abundant diffusion of the Holy Spirit over the people of God, and it will be hidden. The world will be judged in fire and the pouring out of the spirit, the two signs of messianic times. These realties are often presented together, without any chronological distinction: the day of "Yahweh" often means "the day of the coming of the Messiah."

It will be useful to show these different aspects of the Messiah, since we meet them continually in liturgy. Regarding the Messiah, Son of David, it is well to explain the historical and religious importance of the first king who reigned in Jerusalem (the word means, "city of peace," "vision of peace"). The simplicity of David's soul must be pointed out, his dislike of war, his kindness towards his enemies, his human gentleness and his heart which was always available to God. Though his sin should not be left unmentioned (for there were sinners among the ancestors of the Messiah), it must be shown that in him royalty, prophecy and priesthood were united. He was a peaceful ruler (only waged war when forced to do so); he was a prophet, for in his psalms and hymns he spoke in "the name of Yahweh"; and he was also priest (a royal priesthood, different from the priesthood of Aaron) because he brought the Ark to Jerusalem thereby turning it into a sacred city; he also wanted to build a temple. It is in the "new David" that royalty, priesthood and prophecy are intimately joined in the person of the Messiah. The texts of Isaias form here the storehouse between the Books of Samuel to the Gospels.[1] It should be remembered that at the time of Jesus' birth the

---

1. The best biography of David remains the one by L. Desnoyers, *Histoire du peuple hebreu, des Juges a la captivité*, Vol. II, Paris, 1930.

family of David had lost the glory attached to the house of its founder. Both Mary and Joseph, descendants of David, were members of the class of the "poor," that is the *anawim;* Bethlehem had become a small village. This temporary disappearance of the stock of Jesse is profoundly symbolic of the inner and spiritual character of the royalty, priesthood and prophetic mission of the Messiah. Continuing along this line of thought it will further be shown that Jesus, the new David, is King of the *Kingdom of the Beatitudes.*

The expression, Son of Man, means a "being with a human form, but of celestial origin." It should also be pointed out that by itself the expression "Son of God" does not necessarily mean divine affiliation in a strict sense. In the Old Testament Israel is "son of God" under the title of the chosen people; certain texts in the New Testament can also refer to this quality of being chosen; gradually however the term "Son of God" came to signify the filiation of the second person of the Trinity. It is important not to oppose but rather unite the terms "Son of Man" and "Son of God," since both expressions refer to the divine origin of the Messiah.

The theme of *Servant of Yahweh* in certain passages means the people of Israel, but there is no doubt that above all it signifies one of the aspects of the Messiah, namely his redeeming and suffering aspect. At the time of Jesus, Jewish Messianism cared little about the texts in Isaias, at least in their messianic implications; the expectance of the Messiah crystallized above all in a desire for a visible and glorious manifestation of the Anointed of Yahweh. The image of the Son of Man coming out of the clouds and the humble suffering figure the Servant of Yahweh, were fused in the Person of Jesus: "The Son of Man has not come to be served, but to serve and to offer his life as ransom for the multitude."

We should add that John the Baptist, in baptizing Christ in the Jordan, fused the vision of the Messiah, of the powerful

Judge by fire whom he had announced before the baptism of
Jesus, with the picture of the Lamb of God, the descent of the
Holy Spirit in the form of a dove upon Jesus revealed to John
this mysterious link between the power of the messianic King
and the painful sacrifice he was to make of himself. Here, once
again, it was in the writing of Isaias that John the Baptist discovered the Messiah.

The reason we insist on the *messianic, royal, sacerdotal* and
prophetic mission, is because it will recur in the person of Jesus.
The term *prophecy* does not in the first place mean the announcement of future events, but a testimony given in the name of a
person ("pro-fari" or "pro-phemi" means to speak in the name of,
and in the stead of a person, as if that person himself spoke);
the future vision is secondary in the prophetic charism. Re-read
the prophetic function of the Messiah in the testimony of the
prophets of the Old Testament and explain that it was they who
clarified for the chosen people the providential meaning of the
events in its history. The tragedy of the Babylonian exile, in
which the people were "purified," is in the light of the prophet's
preaching one of the chief examples of the role of these witnesses
of God. The "New Exodus" they announced resembles closely
the real "Exodus" or "Passover" Jesus took for the sake of all
humanity.

The priestly functions must be shown in relation to Jerusalem,
the City of the temple. The high priesthood of Aaron appears as
a mediator between the people and the Holy God; but it must
also be recalled that together with Melchisedech and David, a
royal priesthood appears parallel to the priesthood of the Levites.
This apparent contradiction, (for sometimes the Prophets defy a
Levitic priesthood) having at heart chiefly the spiritual sacrifice,
is only solved later through the person of Jesus.

The catechist should keep in mind those ideas presented in
the first volume on the presence of the Holy God in his Temple
above that Ark which is the same time a throne and an altar; the

annual expiation in the Holy of Holies is a forecast of that priesthood about which the Epistle to the Hebrews speaks; the episcopal throne at the back of the apse of cathedrals, the empty
throne above oriental altars (the *"etimasie"* of the Byzantine
art) also illustrates this union between priesthood and royalty in
the person of the Messiah.

As it has already been said, the *royal function* is to be connected with the peaceful rule of David. The rule of Solomon
must be presented as a contrast, humanly more glorious but as
having lost that character of simplicity and love of peace which
marked the figure of David. In illustrating the figure of the
Messiah as King and Shepherd, one should recall how the Prophets cursed the bad shepherd who only cares for his fat lambs
and rules the downtrodden with a rod of iron. Read the admirable parable of the good shepherd in the Book of Ezechiel (Chap.
34) for it forms a link with David who was taken "from his
flock" to become the shepherd of Israel. It also forecasts the
Gospel parable of the Good Shepherd who "sacrifices his life
for the flock." The presence of the shepherds at the birth of
Christ in Bethlehem, city of David, is symbolic of this essential
link between the Old and the New Testaments.

To bring to a close the messianic catechism on the Ancient
Law one should explain the apocalyptic prophecies current before the coming of Jesus. It is essential to explain the literary
genre, above all those which present as one sequence events
which as a matter of fact, occurred at great intervals. The
diffusion of the Spirit, the sign of the messianic times, is an
inner occurrence, for it purifies souls and hearts; but it is visible
too, for it accompanies the glorious judgment of the world by
the Son of Man.

The catechist should gradually pass from the Old Testament
themes to the vision of Jerusalem, the royal city where the
Messiah was to reign, give testimony and sanctify his people.
Here he was to fight the powers of evil and give up his life for

his flock, be resurrected and unite into one single body (which is also the new temple) the dispersed children of Israel. Jerusalem, the city of the Messiah, is also the city where the Church was born on the day of Pentecost.

2. THE NEW LAW

Jesus fulfills all the aspects outlined in the Ancient Law. He is all that; but *above all,* he is more, for his whole person is an unexpected transcendent gift that could by no means be known in advance, but only through the revelation itself. This Person is the incarnate Son of God. Having shown the tension of the Old Covenant towards the messianic revelation, the perspective must be reversed, and it must be pointed out that Jesus is King, Priest, Prophet, Son of David, Son of Man, Servant of Yahweh *because he is the incarnate Son of God.* To make any distinction, to separate in the Gospels the divine from the human in Christ, leads to understanding neither the one nor the other, for they are intimately united. In this sense the divine constantly appears in what is most human, and the human can be found in the very heart of the divine; though the two natures are not confused, they are, however, inseparable.

Jesus is King of the universe, as is God, but he exercises this Kingship through his resurrected humanity. He is a prophet, for he alone speaks in the name of God. Though he is Son of the Father and says only what he hears from the Father, he exercises prophecy by word and gesture, and in the actions of his humanity. He is priest of the Almighty (the Most High). Because he is the Son of God, he is the only one who can offer his Father a holy and perfect sacrifice of infinite merit; however, he accomplishes his priesthood through his humanity which he offers up to the Father "crying in a loud voice, for he learned from his suffering what it meant to be obedient." Jesus is Son of David because his humanity issues from the stock of Jesse whose supreme blossom is Mary, but he is the Son of Man, too, at the same time human and divine, being the incarnate Son of God (in the strict sense of consubstantial affiliation). He is Servant of Yahweh because he sacrificed his humanity like a lamb, but this offering is a perfect service before God, for it comes from the Son of God ontologically united with human flesh. This *coincidentia oppositorum*, this mysterious unity of contrasting aspects in the same personality, should be put foremost in catechism, so that the divine-human personality of Jesus can become apparent. To see in Jesus only a divine myth, or conversely, as the most beautiful among the children of men, the peak of the religious human approach, is to sink into a complete non-understanding of the course of events in the Gospel. Unless it is to be wholly rejected, everything therein must be accepted, including the miracles of Jesus which form an integral part of his personality and his works.

This hidden core of the personality of Jesus is expressed in the New Testament by two essential words: the *Word* and the *Son of God*.

1. The theme of the Word should be followed by the *Image* of the Invisible God. Being the Image and Word of God, Jesus is *creator* and *revealer*, since creation is a word, a manifestation of God, and the preamble to the new creation of the world, the redemption by the New Adam. The literary root of the word *Logos* (which only appears in St. John) is Semitic rather than Hellenistic.

All research made on the Johannine *Logos* agree on this meaning: Christ is the Word, because he is the creative and revealing word which was incarnate. The Greek meaning is secondary; however it is well to remember that for the Greeks this word signifies "the word and the order of the world"; in later patristic writings the fact that the divine *Logos* is present in the world and guarantees its stability, firmness and harmony is important. This explanation is not contrary to the one given in the Old

Testament on the origin of this Word. On the other hand the speculations of Judeo-Christians must be disregarded: although they are not always incompatible with the message of St. John, they may obscure the fundamental biblical meaning of the word. In order to show that the divine *Logos* is at the center of all cosmic harmony, it is better to refer to the texts which occur in the Epistle to the Hebrews: "Radiance of his Father's splendor and the full expression of his being who upholds this world with his almighty word, he has taken his place on high at the right hand of God's Majesty superior to the angels." In this text the link between the theme of the word and the Son of God is apparent; thus the originality of St. John's revelation of the *Logos* can be safeguarded.

The theme of the *image* is a very important one in St. Paul. The most characteristic passage is Col. 1, 15: "He is the true likeness of the God we cannot see; his is that first birth which precedes every act of creation. In him all created things took their being, heavenly and earthly, visible and invisible; what are principalities and powers? They were all created through him and in him; he takes precedence of all, and in him all subsist." The rest of this passage (1, 18), where Paul speaks of Christ as head of the body which is the Church, shows how the theme of the Son of God, word and image of God, creative and regulative word, leads to the theme of redemption in the Church. This link is essential, it will throw light on, and show the faithful as clearly as possible that in the revealed image creation is like a first stage in the theme of salvation.

2. The theme *Son of the Father* (or *Son of God*, these expressions are often equivalent) seems even more important than the former. In an instruction on God the Father, stress the divine filiation of Jesus, a natural filiation in which we participate in the adoption of the children of God. The Gospel text where the Father says "that he is well pleased in his beloved Son," should be put at the center of what Jesus says: "None can know the Son

but the Father, none can know the Father but the Son, and he to whom the Son has revealed him." God's paternity announced by Jesus is no human fatherhood, it is not a composition of philantrophy and benevolence. The Father whom Jesus reveals is the invisible Father who begets his Son, is pleased with him and who remains even in this paternity the Holy God, inaccessible and glorious, whose love can be purification, wrath, consuming fire or the source of the world's transfiguration. In other words it is impossible to know the Father without knowing Jesus.

To go a step further we must attempt to catch sight of the incarnate Son, the prayer in which he continually speaks to his Father, the dialogue exchanged between him and the Father. St. John's Gospel can help us in doing this. We must penetrate into the very core of that inner sanctuary of the incarnate Son, into what Bérulle called the religion of his soul, in order to enter the mystery of Christ. This dialogue not only takes place in the humanity of Jesus; it is already there and is the very life of the second *divine* person (the second *hypostasis,* as the Greek theologians would say) the second divine person is the Son. He is an existing relation from the begotten to the begetting. The fact of the incarnation changes only the mode — essential, however, to us — in that the life of divine relation between the Son and the Father becomes in a way visible to us. Jesus said "he who *sees* me, sees the Father."

What St. Paul said about Christ's affirmative response to God, expresses that the secret of the incarnate second person is nothing but the opening, the forgetting of the self in face of the life coming from the Father. The filiation of a Christian should not be interpreted, in relation to a *juridical* adoptive sonship, but in relation to the natural affiliation of the Son of God. Evidently our own sonship is only a participation of that of Jesus, but at the same time it is more than a mere juridical link, as it is only too often interpreted in accordance with Roman law. When the Christian says his Our Father in and through Jesus, he mysteriously vests himself with something of the filiation of the Son of God. It is only by stressing the life of divine relations between the incarnate Son and his Father, that true meaning is given to the work of salvation, namely turning God's people into children of God. Moreover, when speaking on the subject of the divine filiation of Jesus which was manifested in his Incarnation, it is necessary to beware of the danger of Nestorianism.

There is a lovely passage which illustrates the relationship within the Trinity: "God is humble, not only in the every day trivial meaning, that humility is truth and that he knows himself in truth. But in a far greater and lovelier sense: namely that God does not know himself within himself, that he cares nought for his own glory, that he attaches no importance to himself. The Son does not speak of himself, he does nothing by himself, he knows nothing about himself only what is done by the Father. Whoever sees him does not see him, but the One whom he endeavors, with all his force, to reveal and to glorify, the Father. The Father does not know himself, he does not love himself, he only knows himself well, he only loves himself well in his Son, and every time he manifests himself, he shows us an 'Other,' in whom he is more what he is in himself, the Son, on whom he lavishes all his complacency. And the Holy Spirit does not speak of himself, he says nothing about himself, he repeats again and again enthusiastically, with love and admiration, what he has learned from an 'Other.' Humility is necessary not only to teach us to know man, but also to teach us to know God. Humility gives the taste of God, it is but another name for love." [2]

This life within the Trinity (the "circumincession" of the West, the "perichoresis" of the East), *continues in the life of the incarnate Jesus*. It has become the very heart and soul of Christ, and it is in that life that Jesus will let us participate, as St. John tells

---

2. L. Evely in *Témoignage chrétien*, Belgian Ed. No. of the Epiphany, 1954.

us when he quotes the words of Jesus on the "Father and the Holy Spirit who together with him will come to dwell in the souls of those who keep the Commandments." Moreover, on linking the theme of God's "humility" (which is so profound in Eastern Orthodoxy) to the theme of love, the passage quoted leads directly to the words of St. John, "God is love"; and the words of St. Paul, "The kindness and the love for man have manifested themselves coming from God through his incarnate Son" (Titus 2, 2 f.; 3, 4 f.). When the New Testament tells us that the love of God was revealed in Jesus, merciful sanctification and gratuitous grace are indicated; but the source of this love of God towards men is contained in the life of dynamic relation of the divine persons among themselves; it is present in the eternal filiation of the Son, in the "breathing" love of the Holy Spirit and in the plenitude of which we have received so much.

3. Having thus thrown light on this central point of the person of Jesus, the catechist can now broach the *third theme*, around which the traits of the Messiah can be grouped, the theme of Jesus, the *New Adam*. Christ is the son of David in a profounder sense than the mere concept of the Royalty of David; he is that because he is a man like us, and because in his humanity is joined with his divinity. A New Adam appears who through obedience and redeeming death will beget incorruptible life in us. In the theme of the New Adam we can perceive that "divine plenitude" is bodily present in Jesus, and that through it we, too, can have divine life. The texts on Christ's propitiation for the sin of the world, which has become our "sin," focus naturally on the qualities of the New Adam who by his obedience, contrary to the disobedience of the first Adam, won the mercy of God for us.

The texts of Rom. 5, 12, and I Cor. 15, 45 f., explicitly point out the contrast between the two Adams. A part of patristic tradition stresses the likeness, in that Jesus is a resurrection of the first Adam before the Fall. However, these details can be overlooked in catechism; the central idea remains Jesus, human and our brother because he is the New Adam. Beyond the Davidic lineage, but without omitting it, this theme is directly concerned with the universal character of redemption. By connecting the theme of the New Adam to that of the Word and the Son, we come to the wonderful words spoken by St. Paul concerning the Christ who "recapitulates" all things.

It is important to point out that the word Adam does not merely designate the profane man, a human nature reduced to its purely philosophical dimensions, but human nature as *sanctified and divinized by grace*. What the first Adam should have passed on to his descendants through generations in natural life and divine affiliation, is given us by the second Adam. In other words humanity which the name, New Adam, signifies in Jesus is a humanity wholly consubstantial with ours, but also, and above all, sanctified by grace. The catechist should never forget that the humanity of Jesus was sanctified by the unction of the Holy Spirit, (what later theologians call "created grace"). This sanctity is over and above that infinite sanctity of the Son, this sanctity dwells in us, and informs human nature of the Redeemer. In baptism man is reborn through the second Adam, in the Eucharist he eats and drinks the flesh and the blood of the New Adam. It is in this that the texts of St. Paul on the New Adam who has become "Life-giving Spirit" receive their full meaning.

Adam was created to the image and likeness of God in the sense that the full expansion of his nature, as man, was no mere human equilibrium between flesh and spirit, between body and soul, but an opening, an availability and a conformity, a visitation and a transfiguration of his whole being in the visitation of the life-giving Holy Spirit. The Christ, the New Adam, is a perfect man, not only because there is in him a body and a soul and a spirit (to use the biblical trichotomy), but also and above all because body, soul and spirit are wholly imbued and transfigured by and conform to the likeness of the Son of God. In other words Christ is the New Adam because in him man is *the perfect image and likeness of God;* this image and likeness reach their perfection in him because his human nature is hypostatically united in the person of the Son of God. Our faith and the sacraments give us to Christ and vest us with the humanity of the New Adam, and thus lead us to divine sonship. This is why, when speaking of fornication, St. Paul says to the Corinthians: "Have you never been told that your bodies belong to the body of Christ? And am I to take what belongs to Christ and make it one with a harlot?" Then a little further on he speaks of the presence of the Holy Spirit: "Surely you know that your bodies are the shrines of the Holy Spirit, who dwells in you. And he is God's gift to you..." (I Cor. 6; 15, 19). The close occurrence of these two texts in the same context shows that it is by participating in the humanity of Jesus, the New Adam, that the Christian receives the Spirit of sonship. The Epistles to the Ephesians and Colossians insist on the part played by the body of Christ in our salvation. Finally the Christ, the New Adam, becomes manifest in his resurrection and messianic royalty. The theme of royalty, which is an essential part of Messianism, is here connected to the theme of man, the image of God, that is to say the Lord of creation.

4. The themes of the Word, the Son of God, and the New Adam outline the essentials in the *person* of Jesus. They recur implicitly in a final theme, in *Christ the Lord (Kyrios). Kyrios* surely signifies the all-powerful Jesus, Son of God; but it also implies the tangible manifestation of this power in the glorified humanity of the Savior. The New Adam rules over the world. The catechist must show along these lines the themes dedicated to the glorious return of Christ at the end of time. He can also refer to the Pauline text on the Eucharist which is "the remembrance of the Lord's death until he shall return."

The themes Word, Son and New Adam already contain what is essential in the work of salvation, because the manifestations of the person of the Savior are *inseparable from the work of sal-*

vation itself. We will here deal with the *acta et passa Christi in carne,* as St. Thomas calls the actions and experiences of Christ.

5. The terms "Son of David, Son of Man, Servant of Yahweh," reappear here in their proper contexts, as do the Messiah's threefold mission: royal, sacerdotal and prophetic. These complex themes are united at the moment when the Incarnation of the Son of God approaches ultimate fulfillment at the hour of the Calvary, to *death and resurrection.* By this is not meant that the birth, growth, miracles and teachings of Christ during his life on earth should not be considered in the catechetics, but only that this course should be viewed as a dynamic progress leading to what Jesus called "his hour," "the hour chosen by the Father." This is the hour of the Cross, an apparent victory of the powers of evil, but at the same time the manifestation of the Glory Jesus possessed ever since the beginning of time. It is important to emphasize the paradox of this hour, for in it is reflected the double nature of Jesus, that of the Son of God, and that of the Son of David.

6. The New Testament is so vast that it is advisable to select one central subject to illuminate the entire redemption. The most appropriate text seems to be the one by St. John, which shows that *Christ is our Pasch.* The lamb of God is the real Paschal Lamb who works for us and with us in passage of this world towards the Father, out of darkness into the light, from death to life, from the terrestrial Jerusalem to the celestial Jerusalem. The hour of Calvary is the hour in which God's humanity offers itself in an eternal sacrifice; it is the theme of the Servant of Yahweh. The hour of Calvary is when the eternal victory of God over Satan's power was born. This is also the theme of the *Son of David* who thereby finds his completion. The hour of Calvary is the hour when Jesus is "glorified" by his Father, and through his resurrection enters into the Glory of his Father; it is at that sacred moment of the Paschal night that his humanity begins to

radiate the splendor of divinity and the theme of Son of Man begins to shine in its plenitude.

On Calvary (never to be separated from the Resurrection) Christ manifests himself as *King*, but a king of grief, burdened with the sin of the world. But he is also the King of Glory transfigured by divine life. On Calvary, and also during Holy Thursday night, Jesus offered the Father a perfect sacrifice; he was then fully a priest by the order of Melchisedech. At the end Jesus offered a perfect testimony on Calvary, it was infinite and inexpressible, a perfect testimony to his Father. He was *prophet* in his plenitude, for he revealed in full that God is love and that "there is no greater love than to give our life for those we love."

All aspects of the work of salvation can be found in the picture of the Paschal night of which Egypt was but a forecast. Christ, Son of David, shepherd of his flock, gave himself up for it; he made himself *sacrificial lamb*. But this Lamb of God is also King, and we can see him in the *Apocalypse* ruling over the celestial Jerusalem. The *Servant of Yahweh*, whom Isaias mentions, is comparable to the lamb who is led to the slaughter; and it is in this fact that the reconciliatory *sacerdotal* aspect of the work of Jesus blossoms in the image of the Paschal Lamb. Finally, on the night of the resurrection, Christ, the Paschal Lamb, passed on from this world into another. He became the "prophet of the age to come," and by this fact he accomplished his mission as Son of Man, both celestial (since the Lamb reigns in heaven, and will manifest itself on the last day) and terrestrial (since the Lamb was sacrificed).

The advantage of focusing the work of Jesus on the Paschal night is that the catechist can put the themes of the person of the Messiah into one story; from the Exodus until Holy Week, following up all its stages. In this way he can embrace the entire liturgy as it unfolds. (See further explanation in the chapter on practical suggestions.) The work of Jesus is the peak of the plan of salvation as it was promised to Abraham and realized gradually through the history of the chosen people until it led up to the doorstep of *the true temple,* the one John the Baptist designates speaking of the lamb to be sacrificed for the sins of the world. Finally the catechist must continually emphasize the internal and divine life of the Son of God and Lamb of God, who in his sanctified and sanctifying humanity as a New Adam accomplishes the paradox of the death-life which is the central occurrence of the Paschal night.

The person of Jesus, incarnate Son of God, is therefore the heart of Christianity; here is the basic newness of the apostolic message. Never have other founders of religions put themselves into the center of the universe, none of them has ever said "Come to me." Only Jesus, the incarnate Word of God, could have said, "come to me to go to the Father"; and repeat, as he constantly did, "come to me, take up my yoke, I am the way, the truth and the life." To be a Christian is to believe, it is to give oneself to Christ; it is to live the life of that mysterious being who is both the perfect man, and a God amongst us, the *Emmanuel.*

II. TRADITIONAL AND THEOLOGICAL DATA

A. CONCILIAR AND PATRISTIC DATA

Two phases should be distinguished in the history of theological controversies on the person of Jesus Christ: the first, the Arian heresy dominated by the two Ecumenical Councils of Nicaea (325) and of Constantinople (381); and the second, called "Christologic," marked by the four Councils of Ephesus (431), Chalcedon (451), Constantinople (553) and Constantinople (681). The anti-iconoclast Council (Nicaea 787) was a prolongation of christological controversies.

1. The "Trinitarian" Controversies

The line of *via media,* the golden mean of authentic faith, should be drawn between two opposing heresies, namely *modalism* and *subordinationism.* In face of the Trinity the intelligence is tempted to see in the three persons only three different modalities, three different manifestations of the unique divinity. Against this heresy the Church affirms the existence of three persons or hypostases within the unique divine nature. The opposite temptation is to subordinate the divinity of the Son to that of the Father, so that the former is inferior and even created; this is the Arian error condemned at Nicaea in 325 A.D. with its complementary clause on the Holy Spirit, whose equality in the divinity was affirmed by the Council of Constantinople in 381 A.D. The creed known as the Nicene and Constantinoplean creed or symbol, which is read at Mass, proclaims the essentials of the Church's faith. The catechist by carefully explaining the creed to his students, can connect a good part of the Sunday liturgy to ideas essential to faith.

A balance must be maintained between the two possible extremes: on the one side, insistence on the *"consubstantial"* of the Nicene creed to such a degree that the filial character of the divinity of the Word is lost; on the other to turn the divinity of Jesus into an inferior kind of divinity, e.g. by using terms which imply that the Savior had himself become God, or had progressed in divinity from his birth to his Ascension. Doubtless there had been a progressive *manifestation* of the divinity of Jesus during his humanity, but this progress must be regarded in the perspective of the work of salvation (*quoad nos, non quoad Christum ipsum*). This means that the visible and progressive transfiguration of the Word's humanity makes him gradually assimilative, more communicative towards man. In other words there was a progress in the revelation of Jesus' divinity *to man.* The theophany of the Jordan does not make a humanity divine which is not yet divine, or is only half divine; it manifests to the world the divinity which is present in the human nature, it reveals that it is that divinity which, through the body of Christ immersed in the water of the river, established the supernatural efficacy of Christian baptism.[3]

The origins of Arianism are still obscure. It will perhaps be of interest to point out that recent research suggests that Arianism, far from being a heresy on the Trinity, was originally a christological heresy. In fact the Arian Christology denied the presence of a human soul in Jesus. The Trinitarian heresy was founded on a christological error. The Arians pictured the incarnate Word according to a stoic pattern in which the *Logos* assumed the functions of the soul; from this they deduced that the *Logos* was a created and inferior God who knew the human passions of fear and anxiety in face of death. They pointed out proofs in the Gospel that the *Logos* could have been a *logos ktistos*, Apollinaris, who also denied the presence of an intellectual soul in Jesus while admitting the Nicaean "consubstantial," was supposed to have carried the stoic scheme to its furthest consequences: instead of it being the *Logos* which is an inferior god, it is the "flesh of Christ" which had advanced so far in the orbit of divinity that the expression "celestial man" could be applied. In other words Apollinaris, who was the only true "Monophysite," not only in words but also in ideas, had all but made the human nature of Jesus be absorbed by the radiation of consubstantial divinity, thus abandoning the consubstantiality of Christ's humanity with ours. Notwithstanding this hypothesis, one thing remains certain and it is that one of the chief arguments against Arians is that if Christ is not "consubstantial" with the Father he cannot save us, since being an inferior and created God he

---

3. There nevertheless remains the problem of the "human conscience" of Jesus as it will be seen on p. 180 f.

cannot divinize or communicate to man the divine life which comes from the Father. This is the essential argument of Athanasius and it shows the connection between the "Trinitarian" heresy and Christology. There is no reason why such a simple and biblical argument should not be exposed in catechetics, at least at higher school level.

As for the subject of the progressive manifestation of the divinity of Jesus, we should remember a classical distinction in patristics, now too often forgotten: by it the facts of faith are classified either as "theological" in its strictest meaning or as "economy." "Theology" refers to the mysteries of the Trinitarian life, on the other hand "economy" refers to the scheme of salvation, of the compassionate dispensation by which God has entered into history through the Incarnation. "Theology" and "economy" are distinct but not separated, as we have just seen. They are distinct because (and it is important to see this clearly) the actions and words of Jesus during his terrestrial life should figure in the column of "dispensations," of "communication of salvation" (*quoad nos*), and not in that of the Person, even the Mediator (*quoad Christum*). They are united because the work of the dispensation of salvation is only the communication to the world of the life of the God-Trinity, that is to say the mysteries of "theology." If the difference between the two classifications is made clear it will be easier to make the faithful understand the difference between trinitarian and christological terminologies; one nature in three persons on the one hand, two natures in one person on the other. In this way one avoids the danger of giving the impression that it is a puzzle full of incomprehensible words.

In saying that the progressive manifestations of the divinity of the incarnate Word should be interpreted along the line of the work of salvation as communicated to mankind, it was not meant that human acts and sentiments are a mere delusion, a sort of game (like Marie Antoniette playing at being a peasant

girl in the gardens of Tiranon, as Bernanos puts it) but simply
that Jesus' human psychology and the progress in theophany
should be *first* explained, keeping it in mind that the Word was
incarnate "for us men and for our sins."

2. The Christological Controversies

1. Teachings on the incarnation should center on the Council
of Chalcedon (451 A.D.). Its definition on Christ, Man and God,
"in two natures, one person and one hypostasis" is the rule which
should serve as basis for reading the texts of subsequent Councils;
it is also the result of earlier controversies and of the Councils
of Nicaea and Constantinople and of the Council of Ephesus in
431 A.D.

Between the two heresies, the one attributed to Nestorius,
who all but turned Jesus into a divinized man, and the other,
attributed to Eutychus, who seemed to mix the human and the
divine in a "unique, incarnate God, the Word," the Council of
451 defined the line of Christian attitude. It stressed two points:
the *ontological* (not merely moral or accidental) unity of the
person (or hypostasis) of the incarnate Word, and the integrity
of the two natures, especially of the human nature "perfectly
consubstantial with ours" (except for sin). This truth implies
that Mary is the "Mother of God" (Council of Ephesus). Another
definition which is also a consequence of this truth was set out
by the *Council in 681*, namely that there are "two intellects and
two wills in Christ." They can never be in contradiction, since
the human will always acts "in communion with divine will,"
but they are nevertheless present in a real and human activity
and will in Jesus; this human activity of the Savior is no edifying
play-acting, but real life, passion, death and the resurrection of
the humanity of the Messiah. Finally the condemnation of Icon-
oclasm in 787, extended the realism of incarnation to the icons,
that is to say to all ornamental objects in the liturgical sanctu-

aries; these images are not merely psychologically useful in as much as they concretize the mystery or the person of the saint they represent, but they also have a kind of sacramental value, since by the visible means of line and color, they carry one into the invisible world. They are like windows opening on a celestial Jerusalem. This artistic vision is founded on the dogma of the Incarnation; through the human nature of Jesus the entire material world consecrated by liturgy, enters into the sacred world of sanctified and sanctifying objects.

2. Here are some further specifications which might be useful in more advanced teaching. The definition of Chalcedon will be better understood if the two speculative schemes are kept in mind (strictly speaking it is not an exposition of faith) which divided (and still divides) spirits over the problem of the Incarnation. In ancient tradition, parallel with the scheme Word-Flesh, there is the scheme Word-Man. The New Testament contains the nucleus of this twofold speculative tradition, for example on the one hand in the texts which say "and the Word was made flesh," and on the other, the ones which use expressions as "to assume" "to dwell within," "to come to nothing," to "appear." In both, the unity of the person is emphasized (Rom. 5; 3-4 and John, 1; 14). The history of Christology is ground by these two millstones which are at the origin of two series of dogmatic formulas: those which aim at the duality of the two natures, and those which express the ontological unity of Christ. It suffices to translate into its Greek meaning the word "flesh" in St. John (with him and with the Orthodox Fathers this means *the complete human nature, as contrasted in its own frailty to the power of God*). To see in it a body without an intellectual soul is to lapse into the heresy of Apollinaris. Conversely it suffices to interpret such terms as "assumed" and "human nature" as a nature provided with the quality of a person (in the metaphysical sense), or to translate "assume, dwell in, etc.," in the sense of a moral union between God and the man Jesus to have the Nestorian dualism.

Between the two heresies there is room for the two traditions. While both are Orthodox, one places emphasis on the divine unity of Christ's hypostasis, the other on the integral consubstantiality of his human nature. By a far fetched simplification we arrive at the origin of two christological traditions, the one called Alexandrian, and the other Antiochian.

"It is a well known fact," writes J. Lebon,[4] "that although both stand on the common basis of the New Testament Scripture, the two great theological schools built up two very different christological aspects. The Alexandrian Christology was in the first place, and above all, attached to the contemplation of the eternal Word. Descending together with him from the mysterious heights it saw in the Incarnation only a sort of *episode*, an event of his life and of his own activities. The Alexandrian in no way changed the direct object of its considerations in passing from the Son to the Christ; it was constantly preoccupied with maintaining the absolute unity and identity of the Word with himself before and after the union with the flesh. Antioch, the home of literacy and critical exegetics, maintained a sort of practical rationalism; above all it saw in Christ the perfect man and the perfect God; after the Apollinarian and Arian controversies these Doctors of the Church stressed the duality of the elements in the Incarnation." R. Draguet[5] explains that "the Antiochian theologians insist to such a degree on the perfection of these natures, that they seem to attribute a proper individuality to each, making one person out of each, so much so that the unity they put into Christ seemed a mere pretence to their adversaries."

The difference of emphasis in the two Christologies should be stressed: While the Christology of Severus of Antioch (the father of verbal Monophysitism) is *in re* identical with that of

---

4. J. Lebon, *Le monophysisisme sévérien*, Louvain, 1909, p. 178.
5. R. Draguet, *Histoire du dogme catholique*, Paris, 1941, p. 39.

Chalcedon and Leontius of Byzantium, its point of view is entirely different, since the true formula of Cyril's Christology (which is another, more hardened form of the Christology of Severus and Jacobite Copt and Armenian Monophysites) is that of the "unique nature." The Chalcedonians say that *the flesh of Christ would be part of his normal condition from which he would only be parted in exceptional cases.* For Cyril and the Monophysites *"the flesh is not submitted to humiliations and sufferings, except in particular cases when the Word allows it."* While it is true that the "Monophysites" [6] did not vaporize the humanity of the Word, but "truly introduced the Word into time and history," it must be added that, together with Cyril, Severus also affirms that "the Word transformed his flesh into his glory and his activity." [7]

The words in italics specify the difference in *accent* of the two *orthodox* Christologies which are differently orientated between the two poles in the mystery of the Incarnation. The Alexandrian tendency dominated the Eastern tradition, that of the Orthodox, especially after the Council of 553. It threw light on an essential aspect of Christ, namely the substantial sanctification of his humanity by the divinity which assumes him in a hypostatic union. On the other hand in the Chalcedonian tradition it is not a case of dogmatic formulas *of faith,* but of theological *systems* (which are free as long as they remain this side of heresy) developed chiefly in the West. It must be admitted that the Antiochian theologians, though they never drew up a precise technical formula for Christ's ontological unity (it was Cyril and the Alexandrians who completed this) nevertheless contributed much in clarifying the importance of the presence of a *human soul*

---

6. Wherever this term is in inverted commas it means the partisans of Severus who were only formula heretics in that they refused the Chalcedonian formula, but not *in re,* as J. Lebon demonstrates in his doctoral thesis of 1909.

7. J. Lebon in Chalkedon, Vol. I, p. 559 and 578.

in Christ (as against Apollinaris). The Alexandrians did not
deny the presence of this soul, but their conceptual systemati-
zation did not put this consideration at the center of their thought.

Compared to these Eastern traditions, Western Christology,
from Tertullian to St. Leo, shows a striking synthesis of justice
and balance. This synthesis could be summed up by the two
expressions in the *Tome* of St. Leo (which had a great influence
on the Chalcedonian definition): on the one hand the *agit utraque
substantia quod proprium est* (each substance operates according
to its proper nature) and on the other the *cum alterius commun-
ione* (this action is carried out in communion with the other)
that is to say the human nature only acts in harmony with divine
nature.

These three theological systematizations contributed to the elaboration of the *definition of faith of 451* which reaffirms the hypostatic union in the Alexandrian tradition and the two natures,
without mixture and without separation, of *both* the Antiochian
and Western traditions. The Chalcedonian synthesis was providential, since it united the two poles of the antinomy, the Christology of the divine *Logos* and the one which focuses on the
aspects of the Incarnate Christ. In rising above these speculative
schools, and by giving the formula for faith according to tradition,
this synthesis did not condemn the speculative schools, but reached
beyond them to a higher level. It was at the same time Cyrillian,
Antiochian, and Western. *The definition of 451 was therefore in
no way contrary to the definition of Ephesus.* The disaster was
that the "Monophysites" could not, or would not, see that in
formulas although different from theirs there was the same traditional *faith* to which they too were attached.[8]

3. The Council of 553 should, as St. Gregory the Great stated,
be interpreted in the light of the Chalcedonian Council and not

---

8. J. Lebon, in Chalkedon, Vol. I, p. 579 No. 5 and pp. 389-418.

otherwise; it abolished some imperfect Antiochian formulations which were susceptible of endangering the ontological unity of the Savior.

4. The Council of 681, which partly reaffirmed the decisions of the Lateran Synod of 649, completed the work of describing precisely the meaning of the Chalcedonian definition; and stressed the two wills and two energies of Christ. This Council must be taken as basis for any catechism on the human and divine activities of Jesus, because it will help to point out the essential truth that it is through the humanity of Christ that the Christian should penetrate into the mysteries of the Son of God. Though this Council is too neglected by theologians, yet it is one which throws perfect light on the realism of the Incarnation, the foundation of sacramental realism. The catechist using the 681 definitions could hence explain the important texts of St. Paul: for example, "It was through one man that death came into the world, and it is through one man that grace, too, has come into the world"; "there is but one mediator, that is the man Jesus Christ." The mediation and the priesthood of the Messiah are exercised by his humanity, but he who offers the mediating sacrifice is the *Logos*.

5. Finally the Council of 787 though little known by the majority of the catechists, it gave the essential dogmatic facts which form the basis of all sacraments in the Church (benedictions of the ritual, dedications etc.) which is but an ultimate extension of the realism of the Incarnation. Moreover, Western sacral art has everything to gain by returning to the doctrine on the meaning of icons. Roman art, Byzantine and Roman mosaics and some modern Christian works of art adhere to this artistic trend which "by an invisible method permits us to penetrate into the invisible world."

The transfigured sense of liturgical objects and rituals are derived from this Council, both in the East and in the West. Christians must recover the sacral and sacred sense of religious buildings, objects and rituals; they can only do this if they can see the ultimate blooming of the Incarnation which saves the world, body and soul, spirit and matter, through a truly cosmic grace issuing from the humanity of Jesus ontologically united with the divine hypostasis.

The Chalcedonian definition, together with the three previous Councils, are important. St. Gregory does not hesitate to say that the first four Councils are as sacred as the four Gospels; these words best express the sense of traditional faith. As we have already seen, the mystery of the Incarnation brings us into the presence of an antinomy, the synthesis of which is impossible to perceive *conceptually*. The catechist must, in the spirit of his faith, hold on firmly to the two ends of the sacred chain which God has forged; he must keep a vigilant eye not to lapse into either the Nestorian or the Monophysite errors, as we have already explained in the sociological chapter on Christ. To say that the Incarnation accomplishes in its plenitude *the mystery of love* appears to be the best way of explaining the truth of this mystery. Love wants to communicate its own life; it wants to be embraced by the life of the beloved being; it is ready to be poor amongst the poor, so as to give them its own riches; yet love must remain rich so as to be able to give its wealth to those who have none. "God is love ... he loved this world so much that he gave his Son to save the world," said St. John. The catechist can complete these themes with passages taken from patristic tradition: "God made himself man, so that man might make himself God"; "God who was rich has made himself poor, so that we, who are poor might become rich in Jesus Christ." "Whatever is not assumed (by the Incarnate Word) is not saved." These simple and striking formulas should be memorized by students, for they explain in few words the two poles of Christology: the perfect humanity of Jesus, and the same time in indissolube and inexpressible union of this very nature with the person of the Son of God.

In conclusion, it will perhaps be well to cite the text of the

Chalcedonian definition: "Following the holy fathers we all unanimously teach one and the same Son, our Lord, Jesus Christ, complete in divinity as in humanity, truly God and truly man composed of a reasoning soul and a body, consubstantial with the Father in divinity and consubstantial with us in humanity, similar to us in all excepting sin,[9] begotten by the Father before the centuries according to divinity and according to humanity, born for us and for our salvation, in the end of all time [10] of the Virgin Mary, Mother of God; one and the same Christ, Son, Lord, Only Begotten in two natures without mixture, without change, without division, without separation; for union has not suppressed the differences in the two natures; the attributes of either nature has kept its proper nature and subsists with the other in one person and one hypostatic union. The same Jesus Christ was not divided in two persons, there is but one and the same Son, only Son, God the Word, the Lord Jesus Christ of whom the prophets spoke as taught by the Lord Jesus Christ himself and which the symbol of the Fathers transmitted to us."

All teaching on Christ should end with a devout, prayerful reading of this text, one of the richest in ecclesiastical tradition. The fundamental link with the biblical themes is clearly apparent in it, as is that sense of "Tradition" which is no other than the supernatural instinct guided by the Holy Spirit, by which the Church read and lived the life-giving revelation of Jesus. The definition of 451 describes the inexpressible unity of the divine and the human in Jesus, and the same time points with sober

---

9. This "excepting" sin does not diminish the consubstantiality of Jesus with human nature, since sin does not form part of the "image and likeness" which is the "true" nature of man. Seen from this angle one can understand why the Eastern Churches, while insisting on the transfiguration of the humanity of Jesus, in no way diminished His consubstantiality with ours.

10. These words "at the end of all time" are inspired by the Bible; they show how eschatology commenced with the incarnation.

determination to the reality of each of the two natures. By plunging into the study of these Council texts, the catechist has only to gain, for they are above speculative formulas (however legitimate) and on the plane of the living faith. On reading such a text it is impossible to forget that at the center of Christianity there is a *living* person, Jesus, who lives in his Church.

The devotion of the Sacred Heart, if clearly understood, could put the humanity of Jesus back where it belongs as a "sacrament" of his divinity communicated to the world. It actually bears on the divine love of the Son of God, but incarnate and transcribed, made sensible in the human love of his heart.

B. SOME FACTS OF SPECULATIVE THEOLOGY

1. The crucial problem of speculative theology is to explain how the human nature of Jesus, while not being a human person, is nevertheless wholly consubstantial with ours; in other words the question theologians argue is what constitutes a person. It seems that here it will be necessary to discard the notion of "individuating proper features" and restrict ourselves to *metaphysical* definition: "that which *exists* in itself." In other words, to say that there is only one hypostasis in Christ is to affirm the ontological subsistence of his human nature (including the traits which form his individuality and make him concrete) in a divine hypostasis. The concrete characteristics which make of the humanity of Jesus a *principium quo* which lives and acts (what the moderns call by a word that must be well understood, "a personality," in the psychological sense) do not directly subsist in the "individual quality of the divine hypostasis," but in the human nature; *it is this which subsists, as a whole, in the divine hypostasis.*[11]

---

11. Chalkedon, Vol. I, p. 703, and no. 24 where references to St. Thomas Aquinas will be found.

Some theologians distinguish between the personality (in the phenomenal and psychological sense), and the ontological person. It is perhaps advisable to speak of a twofold knowledge or two consciousnesses in Christ. In order to clarify this point which is important to the catechist, we will quote two texts. The first by M. Browne, appeared in the *Osservatore Romano* on July 19, 1951, explains in what sense one can speak of two "I's" in Christ: "We do not contest the legitimacy of a distinction between the psychological and an ontological 'I.' It depends on what interpretation one gives to such a distinction in general, and in the particular case of Jesus Christ. According to the facts of Christian faith it is clear that one can speak ontologically only of one single personality and one single 'I' in Christ: an 'I' and 'person' which, without any ambiguity are those of the Word in whom the assumed human nature subsists and acts. Psychologically one could speak of the human personality of Christ, but only with reference to the Word, even to the extent where he exists and acts in the hypostatically assumed human nature." The second text reaffirms this distinction while it avoids the danger of falling into the errors pointed out in the preceding text: "Thomism (one should rather say, certain forms of Thomism) might run the risk of falling into Monophysitism, at least on the psychological and mystical plane, to the extent that, while safeguarding the oneness of metaphysical personality in our Lord (that of the Word), it tends at the same time to distrust all the created mysterious vitality that these two little words (as a matter of fact perfectly orthodox) contain, provided they are correctly interpreted: namely the 'human I' of Christ, and the strong 'psychological personality' of the Messiah crucified on Golgotha. Whereas ontologically the assertion of the 'two I's' in our Lord Jesus Christ, is frankly heretical, it becomes admissible and in a way even necessary on the plane of phenomenological description if one keeps in mind the human existence of Christ, which is both natural and *super-natural*. There is no reason to avoid it, because, in comparison with Monophysitism, the human and supernaturalized reality of a *concrete* nature individualized and alive in the soul and body of Jesus Christ must be maintained. In the psychology of the man Jesus there is a complexity and a mobility which in no way affects the immobile plenitude of the simplicity of the divine Word, but becomes necessary for the very realism of the Incarnation. This is only too often forgotten by many of our faithful who are not well informed regarding this point. Beware of the dangers of Monophysitism as well as that of Nestorianism." [12]

2. Without directly entering into these arguments the catechist should always have them in mind and try not to present an abstract and dead picture of the *human* activities of Jesus. Humanity in him is no abstraction, a kind of Platonic idea of nature of the human essence; but the occasion of gestures, attitudes, and words. In brief it is the center of a concrete human behavior which is *psychologically different* from that of any other founder of religion. We must repeat that Jesus was of the Jewish race. The implacable gentleness of Jesus, as stressed by Mauriac, is a universal human characteristic, and can be found in individuals of every race; but it is especially characteristic of the Jewish race. Attention should be also called to the alternating violence and gentleness which mark the behavior of the Messiah. This means that if Jesus is judged against his own background, the abundance of his testimony becomes visible. It will be left to the art of the catechist to describe and concretize the physical aspects of Jesus and try to catch a glimpse of that mysterious element beyond, which is nothing other than the divine life shining through the human gestures. Whether this psychological richness be called a personality, making the distinction between this work and the word person (in the ontological sense), or whether one speaks of

---

12. Quoted in *Ephemerides theologicae Lovanienses* XXVII. (1951) p. 479-480 a propos the texts of Leo of Jerusalem.

a psychological "I" (as distinguished from the ontological I), or whether one speaks (what is preferable) of two consciences and two intellects in Jesus, it remains something that theological speculation does not always succeed in explaining. This is necessary because of the Gospel account. One cannot reach the divine life of the Son of the Father except through his humanity, which is in its turn not just any kind of humanity, but the humanity of the Son of Mary, of the Jewish race, born at Nazareth, at a certain spot on earth and at a certain moment in time with a certain historical background. All the mystery of Christ is contained in these facts which are the psychological human abundance of the man, Jesus, and *the same time* projects on his gestures and words the light of the divinity which dwells in his body. The paradox is in the *ontological union* of the immutable absolute of his divine life with a concrete humanity, the humanity of a Gallilean Jew.

There is a passage by Malègue which describes "the abyss of God's holy humanity": "He took a human body, the human physiology, the economy of poverty, a lower class way of living — his social type was the semi-nomad.

"I heard (Largilier is speaking) this popular sermon in a church in Italy. They were jostling him without knowing him; 'Who's the man over there? It's what d'you call him ... the man Jesus, the son of the carpenter here, you know, the type who preaches down by the fishing boats and in the back gardens. He has some success with strangers, but of course we know him better. Where's he been today? Somewhere down by the lake. He tells his little stories. There's always people who'll listen to him. He made the pigs run into the water. Good thing mine weren't out.'

His categories were of the social class of his country and of his time: the ritual obligations, the penal codes, the forms of capital punishment, the images and the stories of a Palestine Israelite, and he set out his ideas and acts by innocent devices.

He failed. He fell like any other man. Weariness overcame him.

For him, too, stones were hard and beams heavy. He, too, sweated at his work. He sweated the blood of a man in Gethsemane, bled like any human being from the wound of the lance on Calvary. No microscope could find any difference there. He suffered with the nerves of a man all the details of the death of a man; his thirst, caused by lack of blood, the terrible immobility of the cross. He breathed his last breath, as do all the dying.

He suffered from the bitterness of a work shattered by human, the final crushing defeat, the laughter of the masses, the heads shaken in derision, his last hours drowned in ridicule. His mother wept at his feet. He suffered the abandon of his Father, the aridity of the desert and the absolute, a cross on the Cross, a death within death. Accepting the earth meant all of that. He made himself sensible, mortal and very gradually known. I can never contemplate sufficiently the abyss of the *holy humanity* of my *God.*" [13]

3. The catechist should try and show the Redeemer's conscious life — human will, knowledge and love. The texts of St. Paul on the "kindness of God which appeared in Jesus" should serve as thread of the argument to embody this love. The strength of his will and his human conscience must be shown as well as his progress in human knowledge. Try to give a feeling of the co-existence of immutable divine consciousness and all-powerful will of the Son of God, of his consuming immortal and infinite love, the extraordinary mobility, complexity, ardor and vivacity of sensibility, tenderness, and comprehension of the man that he was.

As for Christ's human *freedom*, it is obvious that this must be made consistent with total impeccability. Here is a case of a more profound understanding of the idea of freedom. The soul and will of Jesus are moved by the Holy Spirit, but freely (*autexousiôus*,

---

13. J. Malègue, *Augustin ou le Maître est là*, Vol. II, pp. 486-488.

as the Fathers say); the freedom to choose between good and evil is perhaps (at least according to some theologians, e.g. Maxim the Confessor) but a consequence of original sin. However that may be, if liberty is defined as a *faculty to accept and respond to a divine call,* a soul which is completely open to the divine inspiration would be free in proportion as it no longer belonged to itself, but consented to be totally available. In other words, freedom consists in acting in virtue of a vision of the good by a decision coming from the depths of the spiritual nature; it is the freedom of the elect in heaven. If we apply this to Christ, the very fact that his human will never faltered in face of God, but acted in union with divine will, *constitutes his very freedom.* This is merely a suggestion, but it seems appropriate for penetrating into the depths of the loving dialogue which unites the human freedom of Jesus with his divine will as Son of God.

As for the subject of a possible coexistence of *progress in human knowledge and consciousness* with the omniscience of the Word, several suggest an explanation by comparisons with the lives of mystics. They, too, live in an increasingly profound union with God and at the same time with an apparent dark night of the spirit. The Gospel texts on the agony of Jesus and his abandonment on the Cross could be explained in this sense. It should be noted that although Jesus had the Beatific Vision, he could not practice, in a strict sense, the virtues of faith and hope; he could only do this in a secondary sense.[14] In the difficult problem of the agony of Jesus, we must have recourse to the mystery of love; that infinite perfection of light and of love that wanted to experience the worst human dereliction and suffering of the soul, in order to assume the complete man and to save him. The texts of

---

14. A. Tanquerey, in his *Compendium theologiae dogmaticae* suggests this formula for the *"spes secundum quid"* and makes a comparison with the sufferings of the mystics. See also Chalkedon, Vol. I, p. 178, No. 84 where a text of Leontius of Jerusalem pointing in this direction can be seen.

the Epistle to the Hebrews which refer to "Christ" who learned obedience in the school of suffering and to the fear of death which he wanted to experience so as to liberate man who feared death, must be in the center of all teaching on this subject. This same Epistle is all the more important because it exalts *the divinity* of the "high priest according to the order of Melchisedech."

4. One of the central ideas in Thomistic Christology is *created grace* (together with *capital grace*). A distinction is drawn between the person who acts (the *quod*) and the means by which he acts (the *quo*); we can understand that the divine person does not act directly (*formaliter*) on conjoint humanity, but through the mediation of the unction of the Holy Spirit, i.e. by created grace which in the human nature of Christ is the basis of his sanctity and of his power to sanctify the Church — which is the *Body* of Christ. In other words the *Logos,* being the *principium quod,* assures his ontological subsistence, the foundation of the attribution to one single subject (or supposit) of the acts and words of Jesus, and gives them infinite value. This is why we say "God is born, God is dead"; this is the source of the substantial holiness of the humanity of the Word. Nevertheless the *Logos,* as such, is not the *principium quo* of the human acts of Jesus. The principle of the human acts is the human nature with its faculties sanctified by created grace (and of course linked with uncreated grace). It was thus that Christ had the beatific vision, in which his soul rejoiced and by which his human conscience recognized his condition as the Son of God enabling him to say "my Father and I are one." [15]

The catechist using this Thomistic theme should take care not to separate from its source, the substantial sanctification of humanity through the hypostatic union. It is the same for the sancti-

---

15. The Chalkedon, Vol. I, p. 704; Vol. III, pp. 81-237; Eph. theol. Lov. 1951, pp. 475-476, 481-482.

fication of any Christian; the habitual created grace is a *habitus* which really sanctifies us; but this *habitus* must always be regarded as the result of the divine act of the Spirit in us. *A fortiori,* in the case of Christ both viewpoints must be maintained, the formal sanctification of his humanity through the unction of the Holy Spirit (hence the importance of the part the Holy Spirit plays in the Gospel accounts) and the infinite dignity and sanctity of this same nature through the hypostatic union.

5. Some expressions should be used with reserve, e.g. "theandric activity," "conjoint instrument," etc., since they are easily misunderstood and tend to lower the sense of realism in the human nature of Jesus. One needs great precision of concept to use these words in the strict sense which St. Thomas gives them. If one is not absolutely sure of their use and meaning it is better to abstain from using them.

III PRACTICAL SUGGESTIONS

"To ignore the Scripture is to ignore Christ," said St. Jerome. In the practical field the teacher of Christology should proceed step by step with the Bible. He must do this in two ways, in the text of the holy book itself, and in biblical tradition, that is to say, liturgy.

A. PRACTICAL SUGGESTIONS FOR GOSPEL CATECHISM

The final aim of all christological catechism is to give the faithful a taste of the Gospel, for it is always in its texts that contact with the Lord is the most immediate and has the greatest effect.

It is necessary, therefore, that the catechist himself should penetrate as far as possible into the Gospel atmosphere, so that he may refer to it whenever necessary even in the course of his most technical explanations.

A catechism on Christ without direct reference to the Gospel should be avoided; still less should Gospel texts be used as arguments against any point of Christology. The faithful must be made to realize that the four Gospels are infinitely richer than any technical explanation about Christ. The incomparable values of ancient Council tradition and the liturgy, is that they carry one back to the writings of the Evangelists. The source of all teaching about Christ must be the Gospel, never to be quoted as from a stock of proofs, but treated as an inspiration for the whole teaching.

Precise understanding together with a literal rendering of the texts and their historical background should be fostered. "With the Jew I live like a Jew," were the words of St. Paul; they can be quoted here, for the Christian must find the true appetite for the Gospel message in its historical context. Nowadays every catechist can buy books to help him in this task.

1. The use of the so-called "concordant texts of the Gospels" should be discouraged, because it does not clearly present the life of Jesus. Since each Evangelist has his own originality, it is better to read each Gospel separately.

The Gospel of St. Luke focuses on themes like the power of prayer, the gentleness of Jesus and the universality of salvation. Luke is the *scriba mansuetudinis Christi,* as Dante called him. His story begins and ends in the temple in Jerusalem, showing the author's holy awe and his art in composition. If the four Gospels are read parallel, such treasures disappear.

The faithful are doubtless familiar with the Gospels read at Sunday Mass. Few people ever bother to put these Gospel narratives into their proper context; and still fewer who read the Gospels like they would read a good book. Yet, much could be gained by such a reading. Consider, for example, the two poles of Christology: through the *humanity* of Christ we come to the divinity of the Son of God who leads us to the Father. This is apparent if we read St. John's Gospel in its entirety. His is the most theological account, for it insists on the dialogue between Jesus and his Father. It is also the most human, for the incarnate character of the Messiah is nowhere as clear as in John.

At a second stage of reading, the Gospel should be read with *references to the Old Testament;* begin with the ones explicitly mentioned in the text. Here is one example: the baptism and preaching of St. John the Baptist are presented in different ways (especially by Luke and John). The Precursor announces the realization of the prophetic promises, above all that of Isaias; he preaches in the country beyond the Jordan, in the plains of Moab where the People of God for the last time reaffirm the Covenant with Yahweh before entering the Promised Land. St. John's is "the voice that cries out in the wilderness." This passage comes from Isaias 42, wherein the return from Babylon is presented as a new Exodus, a new passage (this would mean a new Pasch, for the Hebrew word also means passage, leap) towards the Promised Land; it is a more wonderful, spiritual and more final passage than the one from Egypt. Thus, John is a prophet of this new Pasch which is to be completed through Jesus. All these subjects are grouped around the new Exodus which was announced in the Prophets in the context of a new Covenant (Jeremias 31 and Ezechiel 36). The concept of the new Exodus also inspired the Precursor, the last and the greatest among the prophets of the Old Law. He it was who first announced Christ as the founder of the new Covenant in the Holy Spirit.

That these events took place in the plain of Moab on the Jordan shore is another proof that the entry of Jesus into the Promised Land, after his baptism, accomplished the new Exodus. It was also in this desert that Elias was carried to heaven in a flaming chariot, that is to say, when he finished his terrestrial life he entered God's glory. It was in this plain that, after the death of Moses on Mt. Nebo, the people reaffirmed the Covenant before taking Jericho. It was here that Moses and Elias died. This is the link between Elias and the Baptist. For just as the Samaritan prophet was carried up to heaven in a flaming chariot so the Baptist came "in the spirit and with the force of Elias." But there is a still stronger link between Moses, Elias and Jesus; at the Transfiguration on Mt. Tabor it was Moses and Elias who appeared beside Christ. The New Covenant, founded on the death and the resurrection, the pre-eminently Paschal way, was prepared for by Moses and Elias. The Baptist was its precursor, and Jesus its accomplishment. Once this hidden treasure in Scripture has been made clear to the faithful, they can no longer refuse the heavenly manna, far surpassing the wonderful food of the desert.

The principle of a continuous reading of the New and Old Testaments is traditional. For centuries catechism was simply a comment on Bible reading combined with an explanation of the mysteries of the liturgy and the symbols of faith. This *lectio continua* (whose trace can be found in the breviary and the Missal, e.g. during the last three weeks of Lent when St. John is read) formed the core of religious teaching.

2. The next step is to place the Gospel account in its correct geographical position. The faithful will always be prepared to listen to an explanation which locates the Savior in an existing, realistic environment. The paradox must be emphasized in this biblical landscape: poor in art, inhabited by a people which baffles the modern pilgrim just as it baffled the Roman procurators. A tiny country, smaller than Sicily, Palestine is a sort of coastal strip. For centuries great Empires passed through and fought their battles there. It was in this far-flung province of an immense and proud Empire that the Messiah, Savior of the world, was born. The contrast between the great religious mission of

Jesus and the humble environment in which he lived should be clearly shown.

The first glimpse of the Promised Land from Mt. Nebo is *humanly* disconcerting. The pilgrim who read the account of the death of Moses here, is perhaps captivated by the mystery of God's design; but he will also ask how God, who could have chosen any country to carry out his intention for entering history, chose this narrow coastal strip, a land which can only be made fertile by the hardest labor. The paradox of God who "chooses things which are not, to confound the things which are" immediately strikes the pilgrim. If the Christian thinks of Jesus being baptized in the muddy Jordan which flows into an inland sea, enclosed in a desolate wasteland, he will better comprehend the humility of the Savior, and he will realize that he, too, must pass through a sort of unpleasant purification before he can join Christ. This paradox must be emphasized in catechism before the true dimensions of the Beatitudes can be seen. The Holy Land is the land of faith. Its earth is holy, not because the tourist is moved by it, but because "God walked here," a Jew and the son of Mary. The beauty gradually disclosed in this biblical country far surpasses the greatness of Greece or Rome. Whoever has made the pilgrimage to Palestine can never forget it.

One should compare Athens and Jerusalem. Any humanistic teaching in a Christian school which at the end of studies has not turned the students' attention to this dialogue between the two cities, the city of human civilization and the city of the Incarnation of the Son of God would be a failure in Christianity. Films and photographs are easily obtainable, many excellent books contain all the essential facts, and there can be no difficulty in drawing the biblical landscape in order to make the life of Jesus perceptible.

3. Once the geographical background has been illustrated, the catechist should explain the historical and cultural background of Palestine. Explain the political organization of Palestine

at the time of Christ, taking care to refer the Gospel account, the entire Bible and to world history. Unless this is done the sacred story might seem unreal.

Here is an example to make this problem more concrete: Bethlehem, where Jesus, the Son of David was born, is a fertile region where shepherds graze their flocks, as did at one time David, the ancestor of the Messiah. The reigning sovereign at the time of the Redeemer was King Herod the Great. His whole life and his personality reflect cunning, cruelty, megalomania, but also a sense of human greatness manifested in his building; this is the exact opposite of the King of Peace who is to be the Messiah. Herod had his tomb built on the summit of a hill in the desert of Juda (where as a matter of fact he was never buried). It can be seen from Bethlehem, for it dominates the shepherd's pastures as well as the town where Christ was born, and the Holy Innocents were massacred. Explain and show pictures to illustrate this contrast: on the one hand the power of the evil shepherd who "governs with a rod of iron," on the other the simple pasture land and the mild shepherds who were the first to adore the Messiah, son of David. All this will tell more about the "sweet and gentle" Christ than any pompous commentary. If you recall the fact that Herod is remembered only in as much as he had something to do with the birth of Christ, whereas seven hundred million men believe in the Christ, you will have gone a long way in explaining the central mystery of Jesus, the power, the majesty, and the eternal salvation of the God hidden behind lowliness and disregard.

4. Once the general historical background has been presented (do this step by step as you progress with the explanation of each passage), the catechist can proceed to describe the Jewish environment in which Jesus was born. On the one hand the nation was infinitely more religious and pure of heart than ever before the exile and on the other, the expectation of the Messiah was wavering between two opposites: the apocalyptic destruction of

the world, by which the chosen people would gain dominion over the "Goim" or "Gentiles" and a temporal and political Messiah, who would turn out the Romans, restore the power of David, and give the Promised Land independence and wealth. Finally, there were religious factions, quarreling violently between themselves: the Pharisees, austere, meticulous, pious and sincere, but enforcing endless ritual obligations on the poor "of the land," whom they despised; the Sadducees, the great lords, cultivated thinkers, but sceptical especially of the resurrection. Between these two extremes there were opportunists, for example the High Priests, who were anxious to maintain their religious independence and the same time to safeguard the advantages of Roman protection. At the margin of the picture were sects, such as the Essenes, men living in the desert to escape from the corrupt world. Some of these lived northeast of the Dead Sea, where the remains of their monastery and library were found. Moreover from time to time messianic agitators appeared; the most famous of these was one Bar Kochaba, whose signature was found in one of the caves of Aïn Feshka by the Dead Sea.

Against this background the person and the teaching of Jesus immediately strikes one as being paradoxical; Christ accomplished the entire Ancient Law, but passed far beyond it. Jesus had passed between eschatologism and millenarianism, the forms of Jewish Messianism dominating all the hopes of the Jews: at the same time he united these two aspects of messianic hope into one synthesis, his own suffering person who died and was resurrected. It was in accomplishing the prophecy of "the suffering Servant of Yahweh" that he became King and Messiah, he who rules over the world from the height of his Cross, and he who renews Heaven and Earth in the People of God, the true Israel, and in the promise of his return in Glory.

An example can illustrate this viewpoint. St. John tells how Jesus was walking in the portico of the Temple at the time of the Feast of the Dedication. It was here Jesus said that God

had sanctified him and sent him into the world and that the
Father was in him and he in the Father. After an attempt at
stoning him, there followed a dispute. It is enough to place this
account in Jewish religious background in order to understand
the relationship between *accomplishment* and *passing beyond*
which mark the sermons of the Messiah. The Dedication Feast
was celebrated every December 25th to commemorate the third
consecration of the Temple under the Machabees. Innumerable
torches and bonfires were lit in the Temple all along the Cedron
Valley where David's city had once stood. When he said, "the
one whom the Father sanctified," he meant that the true Temple
was his own body; in reproving the Jews for their incredulity,
he alludes to his passion, the hour when the real temple will be
sanctified and will consume and abolish the old. From the same
context the liturgical and sacrificial significance of his death can
be surmised. Finally the discussion with the Jews; who will not
let themselves be convinced, the attention to the tears Jesus is
to shed over Jerusalem and the temple before his passion. This
is the background against which the picture of Titus destroying
the temple and Jerusalem stands; this too was announced by the
Redeemer; it was the decisive sign that the old temple built by
human hands was to be replaced by the new.

   5. a) In presenting the person and the work of the Messiah,
it is well to observe the context with the three different back-
grounds we have presented, but be careful to arrange events in
an ascending order reaching their climax in the *Passion and the
Resurrection at Jerusalem,* the ascent to the Mount of Olives and
the birth of the Church at the Cenacle. The best system is to
combine St. John's sequence of events with St. Luke's; the Fourth
Gospel speaks of several journeys to Jerusalem, the place where
Jesus manifested his glory to the world and entered into conflict
with the Jews. The last ascent to the Holy City is to be shown
in St. Luke whose account of the passion and the dialogues on
the eve of the Passion, from Chapter 9, 51 to Chapter 21, 38

gives an account of this subject up to the Passion. In this way Jerusalem will be always dominating the horizon in the Gospel, as the city of the Passion and the Resurrection, where the Church was born. These are the primary symbols.

b) It is in contact with Jerusalem, — as the place where Jesus came from Jericho, having passed the Jordan for the last time (Jordan, was the river of the new exodus and the new Paschal way), that the catechist is to show the Galilean themes. Jesus had lived and taught during a great part of his public life in the surroundings of the Northwest shore of Lake Genesareth. This was a Jewish region, and the Lord preached mostly to the Jews, but it also bordered on Trachonitis and Phoenicia, pagan countries whither Jesus sometimes went to pray or to find refuge, or else to prepare the Apostles more intensely for their evangelizing missions in the Judeo-pagan world. The catechist should stress three points concerning the Galilean preaching: the happy and prosperous character of the country, a sort of "Galilean idyll"; the poor character of the places where the chief miracles and the greater part of the preaching of the Messiah were performed, and lastly the position of these places along an international trade route, the *via maris trans Jordanem Galileae gentium*, the road from the sea, which ran from Damascus to Egypt, and beyond the Jordan to the Galilee of which the Prophet Isaias speaks in a messianic prophecy. By presenting the picture in this way the littleness of the Kingdom is apparent (the grain of the mustard seed), but also its growth, its openness to world currents within the Roman Empire. There is here a striking symbol of the law of growth of the Kingdom of Beatitudes, beginning from its modest origin to the immense tree in whose branches the birds of heaven nest.

c) Having explained these two themes the catechist should pass on to the three others: Aïn Karin and Bethlehem, then Nazareth and finally Jericho, symbol of the baptism in the Jordan and the temptation in the desert of Juda.

The site of the *Visitation* near Jerusalem (its localization at Aïn Karim is not certain, but the proximity is) will evoke the memory of Zacharias, the priest living in the vicinity of the temple, where every high priest took turns in offering incense. At the same time John the Baptist's childhood can be pictured in the desert region of the Moab and Juda, where he lived as a penitent. Bethlehem evokes the image of the city of David, the shepherd-King, we spoke of above. Point out that Bethlehem is only some four or five miles distant from Jerusalem; thus the cradle of the Messiah was near the city which was to be his grave, but a grave which by traditional symbolism would see the birth of Christ's resurrected humanity.

As for Nazareth, show the humbleness of this small town situated a little off the *via maris*, the sea road mentioned above. Here the true humility of the hidden life of the Savior takes shape. The town is only some thirty miles from the Sea of Galilee; these facts make it easy to imagine the thirty preparatory years of the Messiah. When describing Nazareth speak of the Virgin Mary, of the Annunciation, her life with Jesus and Joseph; of the one and only fountain in the village, now as then. Thus we will present a vivid picture of this humble woman one of the poor, *"anawim"* of the Old Law, who went to fetch water at the well, as the women of Nazareth do to this day. The gentle landscape, the serene village dominating the valley of Esdrelon and sheltered by the valley running down to the plain suggest the happiness of the Messiah's childhood. We picture him as he walked to the synagogue to study the Law, just as any of the other boys of Nazareth. Yet it was Nazareth that gave the worst welcome to Jesus, "for nobody is a prophet in his own country."

In speaking of the regions between Jericho and the Dead Sea, mention the connection between John the Baptist and the Essenes of Qumran—for every now and then we encounter the apocalyptical and the penitential character of the Kingdom. By baptizing all who came to him, John the Baptist surpassed the limits of Essenism. He opened the road of salvation to all, whereas the Essenes remained a more or less esoteric sect. This desert landscape is the scene of Jesus' temptations by the Devil. This geographical and biblical quadrant including the mountains of Moab, the plains of the Dead Sea and Jericho, recall the pilgrimage of Israel in the desert. It was here that the journey to the Promised Land ended; at the city of Jerusalem with its vision of peace. The distance from Jericho to Jerusalem is only 27 kilometers as the crow flies. Jerusalem appears like a keystone at the summit of the undulating hills leading up to it from the desert of Judea. The baptism and the temptation of Jesus are, therefore, connected through John the Baptist with the Mosaic economy of the first Exodus, the first Pasch and the first Covenant.

Jesus' last ascent to Jerusalem in the Passion, the baptism and temptation of Jesus are orientated towards the new Covenant and the new Pasch. Both geographically and biblically Jerusalem is a key point. Thus the sacred meaning of the Holy Land becomes clear. Neither should it be forgotten that both Mark and John begin their account with John the Baptist and the river Jordan; in Matthew and Luke, Jesus' childhood serves as an introduction; the "public life" of Jesus begins at the Jordan shore.

In explaining the ascent to Jerusalem, the catechist should give the picture of the solitude of the desert, describe the road rising from Jericho, 337 meters below sea level, to its highest point at Jerusalem, 785 meters above sea level its highest point. This 1160 meter difference in height is reached along a road haunted by robbers; it illustrates the difficult journey which was to be Jesus' last before his Passion. The completely arid country suddenly changes into a mild, almost Tuscan, landscape at Bethany on the eastern slope of the Mount of Olives. This was the place where Jesus stayed with his friends during that Holy Week.

When describing the Mount of Olives, one should call to mind the tears Christ shed over Jerusalem, the city which stoned and killed the prophets. From here the view of the Holy City dominated by the Temple is incomparable; and yet, as Jesus said "not a stone was to be left on another." Recall that it was in this place that Christ pronounced the great apocalyptic discourse (read in Matthew) announcing the replacement of the carnal Israel by a new Israel, a new People of God in the spirit. The faithful would understand once and for all the tragedy of Jewish unbelief and the deep wound it left in the heart of Jesus and his Church. If the catechist shows that according to ancient tradition, the Messiah taught the Our Father (to be repeated and commented upon) to his disciples at this place; he can tie the ancient Jerusalem to death. In this way the students will understand how with the Church (the New Jerusalem), they enter into the eschatological Kingdom of the Glory of the Father.

Subsequently the catechist should describe the Valley of Cedron which lies between Jerusalem and the Mount of Olives. Here Jesus suffered his agony and was arrested in Gethsemane, the garden at the foot of the hill. There is a symbolic meaning in the fact that in this valley are scattered Jewish and Moslem tombs. The pious Jews desired to be buried here, believing erroneously that it was the place for the resurrection of the dead, that is why they called this valley cemetery, the valley of Josaphat. The Moslems believed that a mighty prince, perhaps *Jesus himself*, is to pass through the "Golden Gate" which faced the Temple porch, on the last day to announce the resurrection of the dead who lie facing the Temple. These traditions illustrate the connection between the Valley of Cedron, where the Messiah suffered the anguish of the fear of death, and the hope of resurrection — the essential fact in Christian faith.

In describing the city of Jerusalem, the teacher should paint the fierce aspect of the city perched like an eagle's nest in the mountains, which seems menacing the citadel of Zion. This temple-city was the target for the aspirations of the Jews of the Diaspora, and the meeting place of mountain tribes who assembled there to ascend to the house of God. In this cruel, foul and miserable cosmopolitan city, amidst the many passions of the men of his time, Jesus was condemned and died. It was from this narrow cradle that he emerged by his Resurrection. It was in the heart of this city, which had stoned its prophets, that the Incarnate Word laid the foundations of his Church in the Eucharist. This was to be that terrestrial Jerusalem, militant and suffering, animated by the life of its divine Spouse, and also the heavenly Jerusalem, triumphant, and resurrected, free because the Calvary is only a few paces distant from the tomb out of which the *Lord of Glory* emerged on Easter night.

Continuing with the description of the Mount of Olives, the catechist can evoke the Ascension of the Savior, the prelude of his return to us in the Spirit. Rising from the sea a strong breeze blows over the hilltops at dusk; it recalls the words Jesus spoke to Nicodemus, the "wind which breathes where it will, thou canst hear the sound of it but knowest nothing of the way it came, or the way it goes."

Before telling the account of the Ascension the catechist should once again briefly illustrate the life of Jesus. Three quadrants will suffice, one of the hills of Judaea, between Jerusalem and Jericho overlooking the Dead Sea and the plains of Moab for a distance of some 27 kilometers. This recalls the Old Testament and the biblical and geographical preliminaries. It was here that John the Baptist lived. Secondly one should present the image of the Mount of Olives where the Ascension took place, the summary of Jesus' historical life in its plenitude, the entry of his humanity into the Glory of the Father, and the announcement of his return at the end of all time, to judge the living and the dead. Thirdly, a view of the city of Jerusalem should be presented in order to remind us that man is not an orphan, not abandoned by Jesus; for over the horizon there always shines the vision of the Cenacle, where the Eucharist was instituted and where the Church was born on the day of Pentecost. Jesus has thus come to live amongst us through his Church, through the Holy Spirit; in the sacraments and the Apostolic hierarchy.

Finally the catechist can add to his biblical and geographical descriptions some ecclesiastical details regarding the growth of the Church. He can point out Damascus, the thousand year old city, the connecting link between Egypt and Mesopotamia; the place where Ananias met with St. Paul and baptized him, thereby turning him into the Apostle of the Gentiles. One can speak of Cesarea of Palestine, where St. Peter baptized the first pagans, where St. Paul stayed two years before he came to Rome, and where there is still a pier built by Herod, the bad shepherd, who appeared at the dawn of the life of Jesus and of the Church here in this Mediterranean port opening on Rome, the *Cathedra Petri*.

As for Galilee we can add that in the evangelical scene of the Beatitudes, this entire region appears like a new Zion, the site where the New Law was promulgated. Our Lord keeps repeating the words "it has been said to you, but I say unto you." Personally, we think it better to place the Transfiguration, which is a hinging episode between the Galilean idyll and the Passion, on Mt. Hermon. In fact the promise made to Peter (Mt. 17) immediately after the Transfiguration, takes place in a pagan region in the foothills of the Hermon. Since the Church is universal, the founding of the Church on the "rock" of Peter therefore takes place on pagan ground. If we locate the Transfiguration on this mountain which dominates the landscapes, the life of the Church as of Christ will appear in the light of the Passion and the Resurrection under the sign of the paradox of the death-life.

B. PRACTICAL SUGGESTIONS
FOR A LITURGICAL CATECHISM

The Syro-Palestine corridor, the stage for the story of salvation, though a mere strip of land was exposed in all directions to the surrounding countries. Similarly the story of Jesus, though it was hidden from the eyes of the world, was open to the universe. In the same way, liturgical texts and ceremonies for all their humbleness have the potential power of the resurrected Christ. In them we find the dialectics which unite the two Testaments; but amplified by ecclesiastical tradition, and connected to the Gospel texts which we have already pointed out in the preceding suggestions. In other words the teaching of the Gospel is pivoted on liturgical catechetics, which is simply the Bible as prayed and lived by the People of God together with Christ who is present in all the sacraments of the Church.

The subject is automatically divided into two parts: the Christmas to Epiphany cycle, with the Advent preparation, and the Easter-Pentecost cycle, with the Lenten preparation. In a certain sense the first cycle is complete in itself, for it contains the introduction of the redemption, and in a way anticipates its realization. But the Pascal cycle came first in time, and it was only after the celebration of the Sunday that its liturgy was elaborated, first focused on the Resurrection, and only later on the Nativity.

1. THE CHRISTMAS-EPIPHANY CYCLE

1. The Advent season should be presented as focused on what is called the three types of Advent: Mary as the central type; Isaias, "the Evangelist of the Old Testament," at one side, and John the Baptist, the Precursor, at the other. The three advents of the Messiah, in the body, in the heart of the Church, and at the end of all time, should be explained with reference to Isaias. The catechist should describe Mary as the supreme flower of the ancient law by the twofold movement indicated throughout the Bible, the one by which God descends towards men (*Rorate coeli desuper et nubes pluant justum*) and the other, which gradually prepares the earth for the cradle of the Messiah (*aperiatur terra et germinet Salvatorem*) and reaches a mysterious juncture

in the Virgin. In her, therefore, the fullness of faith should be stressed, her acquiescence in the words of the Angel; in her "the earth opens," in her the Lord of Glory is incarnate. Finally in the figure of John the Baptist, the catechist should show the key position of Christ's forerunner.

It is essential to teach the three advents of the Messiah, for often Christian piety stops at the Crib, and rarely goes beyond the vision of Jesus' incarnation in his Church, and finally nearly always forgets his last coming, at the end of all time. The Messiah has come, and we no longer await him as do the Jews; but also he has not yet come, and we await his glorious arrival. The tension between these two comings gives the essential character to the whole atmosphere of Christian life, situated within the stretch of time between the Resurrection and Parousia.

The catechist should emphasize the importance of the Precursor's role, and point out that he is mentioned in the *Confiteor* together with Mary, the Apostles and the Saints.

2. Once the "three types" of Advent is sketched in, the catechist can outline the principal points of the Mass, as they are revealed in the Missal. The best way to make this teaching concrete is to comment on the great antiphons, unsurpassed in theological richness. The great models of the Old Covenant are reaffirmed and applied to the Savior of the world; in this way a certain sentimentality of some Advent sermons can be avoided. Here the Messiah appears as *Wisdom*, creator and revealer, as *Lord* leading the People of God, as descending from *the line of Jesse*, raised like a sign above the nations, like the *Key of David*, who alone can open the prison doors of sin and death, like the *Orient* whose light comes from God and will illuminate the man sitting in the shadow of death, like the *King of Nations and Cornerstone* which will unify the world, and lastly like *Emmanuel*, God with us. It is enough to run through these antiphons to find the titles of the Messiah — Son of David, Son of Man — that emphasize the divine power operating in the Savior.

As a practical piece of work the students could be asked to go through the texts of the Missal and find the three types of the Advent and the chief characteristics of the Messiah as announced by the Prophets. It would suffice to point out the main themes; the texts should be classified accordingly and a central synthesis drawn up. Obviously the same kind of work can be done for all the liturgical seasons. If treated as team-work, each student giving his own viewpoint, this work could prove even more useful in teaching how to connect catechism with the Missal, i.e. with the ecclesiastical celebrations of mysteries. Often this will urge a keen student to read Isaias and the first chapters of Luke and Matthew; the student may then be tempted to re-read the Bible, this time in the light of Church tradition. It is easy to complete this work by searching for reproductions of works of art on the principal aspects of the Advent. Experience has shown that this system of working has often proved revealing for the student.

3. The feast of Christmas is to be presented together with the Epiphany. A useful method is to focus teaching on two poles: the manifestations of the Son of God to the world, and the mystery of God's espousal with humanity. The texts of the three Christmas Masses, whose origins must be explained, keeps intermingling the appearance of divine goodness and the divine grandeur of the Son born of the Father before all time with the humanity of Jesus. The chief Mass, the one on Christmas Day, underlines both the divine and powerful character of the Child who "is born unto us," and the light of Glory and Salvation radiating over the universe. The glory surrounding the shepherds of Bethlehem in the holy night, the Angel of God who appeared to them, the hosts of singing angels are all directly linked with the glory of God present amidst his people under the ancient Law.

Presented in this manner the feast of Christmas is spontaneously attached to the Epiphany, which contains three famous mysteries: the adoration of the Wise Men, the baptism in the Jordan, and the wedding at Cana.

Baptism in the Jordan sanctifies the baptismal water; the Spirit, who takes under his shadow the humanity of Jesus, "regenerates" the baptismal water and turns it into life-giving water (just as it brooded over the waters of primordial chaos). The Father who manifests his Son indicates that the Messiah should lead us to him; finally the baptism of Jesus is the "nuptial bath" in which the Church (which is the extension of the Savior's humanity) purifies herself in order to participate at the messianic wedding. The feast of the wedding is presented in anticipation by the miracle of Cana; the water changed into wine is the symbol of the Eucharist and of Baptism; the hour of Jesus is anticipated figuratively, and the Savior's glory is manifested to the disciples. At this wedding feast the three Wise Men, symbols of pagan nations, "come hurrying with presents," for the messianic banquet is to unite all people in one eucharistic meal.

With the Epiphany the coming of Christ is achieved, and yet not achieved, for we are still awaiting the glorious coming of the Messiah for all humanity; and we await him together with the Church, in faith and hope, vivified by the divine life of the Savior. The fact that in some countries the feast of Epiphany is no longer celebrated as a holyday has resulted in an almost total forgetting of this solemnity; teaching about the Epiphany too, is only too often limited to the mention of the three Wise Men whose purpose should, however, be interpreted in the light of the two other mysteries of this feast (which takes place in eight days on the second Sunday after Epiphany). This situation should be remedied, attention drawn to the fact that the Sundays from January to Septuagesima are called "Sundays after Epiphany," in the same way as the Sundays after Pentecost, of which they are a sort of preparation. They have an ecclesial and eschatological aspect, i.e. in the Gospel texts separating the cockle from the wheat and on the grain of mustard seed. The catechist is advised to begin his teaching on Christmas as from the mystery of Epiphany.

What has been said about the three mysteries of Epiphany can be found in the antiphons of Lauds: "Today the Church has been joined with her celestial spouse, for Christ has washed her sins in the Jordan. The three Wise Men came to the royal feast bringing their presents, and the guests rejoiced in the water changed into wine." In this admirable antiphon the theme of the manifestation and of the espousal is strongly apparent. Having explained all this, the catechist can pass on to the feast of Christmas, stopping at the antiphons of the feast of the first of January and especially at "the admirable exchange which took place in the Virgin" this exchange which "gave us with liberality the Deity." These antiphons of Greek origin give with sober lyricism the dogmatic truths defined at Chalcedon; they put the Incarnation under the sign of the communication of the life of God on earth. It should be added that the celebration of the first of January is probably the oldest feast of the Virgin Mary; it underlines the role of the Mother of God in our salvation.

The feast of Christmas will then appear in *all its messianic amplitude*. It is well to remember that the *Gloria in excelsis . . . et pax hominibus bonae voluntatis* means Glory to God in the highest and peace on earth to men *whom God has loved*. This interpretation is infinitely more profound than the one usually given, by translating "men of good will," since it signifies that peace, the espousals have been achieved between the inaccessible Glory of the Father and the humanity which God loved, loved so much that he did not hesitate to give his own Son to save it. At the same time the link with the Old Law appears in the announcement made to the shepherds. By this the faithful will easily understand how the human theme of the Crib is interlaced with the virgin birth from Mary and the birth before the dawn of time from the bosom of the Father. Hence the royal and divine aspect of the Child born at Bethlehem can be developed, for it is strongly emphasized in the liturgy of December 25th, above all in the texts of Isaias.

The feasts of the "Holy name of Jesus" and of the "Holy Family" are to be shown in this light; not the other way around, reducing the mystery of Christmas-Epiphany to these narrower perspectives. It is not a question of diminishing the importance of the devotion of the humanity of Christ, e.g. with regard to the Crib, but only of putting it back in its original place.

The feast of the Purification, on the second of February, falls in the extension of Epiphany; it celebrates both the consecration of the Temple of Jerusalem by the coming of the *glorious* Messiah, as it says in the text in Malachy; and also it replaces and transfigures this ancient temple into a new temple, into the body of Christ which is to be offered for the salvation of the world in a "pure oblation." The candles the faithful carry represent the messianic light shining over the nations: they represent the faith in which the People of God (whose supreme flower is the Virgin) go to their Redeemer. This feast closes the Epiphany and at the same time anticipates the mystery of the Paschal sacrifice which it celebrates in the following cycle.[16]

We suggest the following regarding the devotion to St. Joseph. The Latin liturgy connects Joseph, Mary's husband, with Joseph of Egypt; the Eastern liturgy adds a comparison with Joseph of Arimathea who gave his grave for Christ's body taken down from the Cross. Joseph of Egypt was not one of the men who announced the messianic message, for this was "set" for Judea, but a protector of his brothers, he also safeguarded the temporal cradle of the Savior's race. The "Father" of Jesus, warned by the angel, saved the Child from the massacres of Herod by fleeing to Egypt. Finally Joseph of Arimathea gave the crucified body

---

16. For all this see the Jan. No. 1954 of *Vie spirituelle;* see also *Revue Nouvelle*, Dec. 1952 and *Epiphanie à refaire* in *L'actualité religieuse dans le monde*, No. 10, Jan. 1st, p. 1-2. All that has been said of the feast of Jan. 1st, said to be the oldest feast of the Virgin, has been suggested in a course on liturgy, by D. B. Botte.

his own grave, that is to say a temporal cradle wherein the Lord "slept" buried for three days. It seems that the role of St. Joseph, patron of the universal Church, should be interpreted in the same sense; he is the *temporal* protector; this aspect will suit the devotion of many faithful who ask St. Joseph to procure them the temporal help which they need for their good works.

2. THE EASTER-PENTECOST CYCLE

The preparation for Easter is divided into three periods: first the Sundays of Septuagesima, Sexagesima, Quinquagesima; then the four Sundays in Lent, and finally two weeks of Passion which terminates with the Holy Week, which is entirely in the light of the Paschal mystery.

A. THE PASCHAL PREPARATION

The three Sundays before Lent remind the faithful of the Fall and the promise of Redemption. On Septuagesima the Creation, the Fall and the Promise made to "the descendants of woman" is to be recalled. Read once again what has been said in the chapter on God on the subject of creation regarded as one step in the work of salvation, and Redemption as a new creation of man. At Sexagesima recall Christmas and the deluge, taking care to emphasize the baptismal and ecclesial symbolism of the Ark. Quinquagesima is to focus on the figure of Abraham, the Father of all faithful, the model of the man who has faith in the promise to the extent of a willingness to sacrifice his only Son, the Child on whom the realization of God's plans depended; the connection with the sacrifice on Calvary is here indispensable, it is as a matter of fact reaffirmed in the Paschal liturgy. The mysterious grandeur of the texts in Genesis, read during Lent and followed by the entire Pentateuch, immediately puts the Redemption in a cosmic perspective, and at the same time it brings the picture of the Church into the history of the chosen people.

2. The spiritual life in Lent is to focus on *prayer, fasting* and *alms-giving*. The catechist is to explain that prayer is above all the intense reading and meditating on the holy books, for each day a proper Mass is proposed to the faithful; he is to add that fasting should be above all a fasting from sin, as said the Prophet Joel, who preached about penitence in preparation for the day of Yahweh; finally he should explain that alms are not a mere giving of material values, but also of spiritual values; e.g. by telling our brothers of the charismata we have received.

These Lenten virtues are to be put into the picture of Jesus' penance in the desert, and his transfiguration. The number forty can be compared with the forty years Israel lived in the desert, the forty days Moses spent on Mt. Sinai and the forty days Elias travelled until he reached Mt. Horeb. The communal character of Christian penance is thus compared with the pilgrimage of God's people in the desert (the prophets always said that it was there that Israel was purest and nearest to God), and whither our brother Christ retired. The catechist should finally draw attention to the connection there is between these facts, the river Jordan and the Red Sea, viewed from their baptismal aspects; this is also characteristic of Lent, since it prepares the faithful for a revival of his own baptism in Christ's death and his resurrection with him. Do not forget the ultimate preparation at the Christian initiation of the catechumens. The transfiguration celebrated on the second Sunday in Lent completes the picture wherein all celebrations are in the light of Joy, which bathes Christian asceticism "under the shadow of the wings of the Almighty," as it says in Psalm 90, the pre-eminently Lenten psalm.

3. The period of Passion extends and transposes the previous themes by focusing all aspects on Jesus, light of the world, in conflict with the forces of darkness, the suffering righteousness

of whose coming and grandeur the Prophet Jeremias sang (to be read parallel). The liturgy of this period is completely christological, it reveals that the two preceding periods have no other meaning than to unify the faithful to the death and the resurrection of Jesus.[17]

B. HOLY WEEK

Beginning with Palm Sunday the Church follows step by step the last hours of the life of Jesus. Recall once again from this aspect all that has been said on the teaching of the Gospel regarding the ascent to Jerusalem. Liturgy evokes these events, both as historical facts and as sacraments of salvation.

1. The catechist should begin with Palm Sunday and point out its double aspect: the triumph of the King of Peace who enters the temple in Jerusalem (here the voices of the children symbolize the angel voices acclaiming the resurrected Christ who enters into the heavenly Jerusalem); and the desolation of the tragedy of Passion which dominates the Mass on this Sunday. This Sunday is (as a matter of fact every Sunday is) an Easter, but Palm Sunday especially, because the contrast between the luminous and fresh glory of the entry into Zion, and the grief of the Passion is more strongly marked. On Monday, Tuesday and Wednesday details of Jesus' last hours should be re-read; Bethany, the eschatological discourses, the discussion in the Temple; all this is dominated by the account of the anointing in Bethany and the reading of the Passion in Mark and Luke.

---

17. All this can be made more clear by reading in *Cahiers de la Roseraie*, Vol. I and II, Ed. Lumen Vitae and the Abbey of Saint-André, 1952-1953; written in collaboration these works propose themes on Lenten catechesis. The basilicas where the Stations are held are also a source for inspiration, as it has been suggested in *Lumen Vitae*, V. (1950) pp. 671-677.

2. The essential thing is to make it clear that the three days of Holy Week, Thursday, Friday and Saturday, form one single mystery.[18]

a) It is useful to begin with the aspect of Good Friday, at least in cases where catechesis is not linked, e.g. in parish preaching. Friday is the day when the Son of God became entirely similar to us; he had then achieved the full human condition, since he came to know death and burial. But it would be a mistake to limit ourselves to the humanly painful aspect of the Passion; Good Friday liturgy has in fact a triumphal character, above all in the exaltation of the Cross, on which it centers.

On this day the liturgy is fully focused on the adoration of the Cross; the prayers and chants which are its preparation reproduce the ancient liturgical synaxis; the chanting of the Passion, according to St. John, is filled with love, human grief and the feeling of the glory of the Word. As a matter of fact almost all of this Gospel is read during the three weeks before Palm Sunday. The great orations which originally followed the *Oremus* of the offertory on every Sunday manifest the sense of universal Redemption of this glorious Passion which is a *sacrifice*. Read in their own contexts the preparatory ceremonies which culminate in the adoration of the Cross, the singing of the *Improperia* recall for the last time the long story of the faithlessness of the People of God and the fidelity of God in them; the *Pange Lingua* brings the tree of the Cross near the tree in the Garden of Eden; the source of death through Adam has now become the source of the resurrection and glory through Jesus, the New Adam; the antiphon *Crucem tuam* and the *Vexilla regis* announce the joy of the resurrection and remind us that it is from the height of his triumphant Cross that the Messiah is to govern the world.

---

18. The classic to be read is L. Bouyer, *Perennial Liturgical Piety*, Notre Dame, Indiana, 1955.

The "Paschal passage" is thus clearly apparent in the liturgy of Good Friday [19] and we participate in it by the communion.

b) The liturgy of Holy Saturday is a vigil; throughout the night of the resurrection, as at the time of the escape from Egypt, *the Christians keep vigil,* that is to say they are united in watching over "the passage of God amidst his people"; they die and are resurrected together with him. In this night of Easter the Messiah becomes the cause of our salvation, for his death defeats death, so that to die with Jesus (first die to sin, and then die to this life) is to resurrect with him. Baptism is the sacrament of this passage, but it is crowned in Christian initiation by the sacraments of Confirmation and the Eucharist. *Per crucem ad lucem,* these words manifest the indissoluble oneness of Good Friday and Holy Saturday.

All this can be explained in a catechism on the rituals of the Paschal vigil. The fire lighted and blessed at the entrance of the Church is at the same time the symbol of the light of Christ and of the love of the Holy Spirit. The Paschal candle, lighted beforehand, which precedes the procession as it enters the dark nave, is the symbol of the shining cloud which led Israel across the desert; but also it stands for Jesus' humanity in which lives the flame of his filial divinity. As the procession of "the People of God" approaches the choir, the number of lighted candles multiply; as it approaches the Promised Land, the terrestrial and celestial Jerusalem whose symbols are the altars, God's light waxes and shines with the clarity of faith and the warmth of love. The singing of the *Exultet,* crowns the first part of the vigil by evoking the "holy night" when God saved his people; it commenced with the great night of the Exodus, the image of Christ as the Paschal Lamb. Here joy reaches incomparable heights and culminates in

---

19. See on the history of Good Friday rituals, B. Capelle in *Questions liturgiques et parossiales,* December 1953.

the unforgettable, holy and audacious *felix culpa quae talem ac tantum meruit habere Redemptorem.* Every Christian should learn by heart this song of the people saved from death.

Reading from the Old Testament which follows recalls by way of preparation to Christian initiation some of the great stations in God's design, such as the creation, the deluge, the sacrifice of Abraham, the Exodus, etc. Thus the Resurrection of Christ appears closely linked with the sacraments of salvation.

The benediction of the baptismal font brings us to a dialectic which culminates in the Mass and in the communion of the baptized people who will be resurrected together with the Son of God. The blessing of all baptismal waters evokes in sovereign grandeur all the waters which, from Creation to the Jordan, from the Red Sea to the baptismal fonts, saw either the shadow or the real salvation of the world. All the teaching about baptism should be focused on these texts. The Paschal candle dipped thrice into the water of the font represents the descent of God into the reality of this world in order to sanctify it through *his holy humanity.* The holy oil and the holy chrism, which the priest adds to the water, represent the Spirit which communicates life and consecrates the People of God in a royal priesthood. The baptism, which can be conferred, as desired in the Rubrics, the renewal of the baptismal wishes in common, introduce the Christian assembly to the mystery of life and death. The Easter Mass which terminates the celebration, represents the reality in this messianic banquet; its first sign was the marriage at Cana; henceforth the faithful possess in their own persons the pledge of the Kingdom, to come; they are armed with faith and hope, they can await the return of Christ in his Glory. The Lauds, which close the vigil, sing of the new day "which has no end."

c) Thus the Son of God has become consubstantial with the world; he is also the only cause of its *salvation.* But it is yet necessary that this cause of salvation be assimilated to the world; it is indispensable that every man be able to "eat the flesh and drink the blood of the Savior"; it is necessary that God offer with Christ and in him the oblation of sacrifice which will take away the sin of the world. Jesus made this last communion of himself in the night of Holy Thursday in instituting the Eucharist. It is thus that the third mystery of the Paschal aspect appears inseparable from the two others, but linked with their ecclesiastical continuation.

The Mass *in Coena Domini* evokes the holy Cenacle where Jesus ate with his disciples; it is the announcement of the death on the Cross; it announces the return of the end of all time; it is connected through time and space with every Mass, and the same time it is the center of all sacraments and sacramentals of the Church.

The essence of these rituals is steeped in an atmosphere of love, of incarnate charity in Jesus as he washed his disciples' feet. The *agape*, which is the very heart and very soul of the "Paschal time," appears in the Gospel and in the following *Mandatum;* this is a ceremony enacting a parable of the Passion. The Eucharist is a non-bloody offering of the bloody sacrifice of Good Friday; it is its ritual offering.[20] It is also communion with the Body and Blood of Jesus who brings our body *the ferment of the resurrection;* it is the memory of the gesture of the Savior and conveys his sacrificial humanity united with the person of the Word; it is at the same time a pledge of our expectation of the glorious return wherein the decisive word is the *donec veniat* of St. Paul. At all events its eschatological meaning should be emphasized, otherwise the close link between the mystery of Holy Thursday with the Pasch, the Ascension and the Pentecost would not be apparent.

A second aspect of this liturgy is its reference to the Church, which was born from the side of the New Adam, asleep on the

---

20. We remain faithful to the theory of M. de la Taille in *Mysterium Fidei,* whose theology is so close to liturgy.

Cross; the blessing of the holy oils and the holy chrism, which takes place during the morning Mass in the cathedrals show that all the sacraments and sacramentals of the Church are only an extension of the Word's humanity offered up on the Cross in his Resurrection and given as food to the world. The catechist should explain some of the ways the holy oils and chrisms are used, e.g. baptism, confirmation, ordination, anointing of the sick, dedication of a church, benediction of church bells, etc. He should make it clear that all this is but the "sweet fragrance of Christ," the unction of his spirit which is diffused from Calvary in the form of the Eucharist over the whole world. He should also insist on the fact that every year, in every diocese, the holy oils and the chrisms of salvation are blessed anew by the bishops who are Vicars of Christ and successors of the Apostles, in order that from this height "the oil of exultation" may gradually descend "into the beard, the beard of Aaron." Thus every parish baptism, every confirmation, etc., has its roots in the holy humanity of the Word, communicated in the Church through the Spirit.

A more advanced catechism could add to the commentaries on the *Triduum sacrum* a brief explanation of the three days preceding Easter. That of Maundy Thursday focuses on the anguish of the Savior who is to be betrayed by one of his own disciples; Friday rings with the cries of pain and the struggles of Justice suffering in his Passion; Saturday is bathed in the light of what might be called "the vigil of the divinity"; around the tomb of Jesus the holy women watch and the Church with them, knowing that he who is buried there "sleeps" awaiting Resurrection (the word cemetery means "place for sleeping" hoping for the resurrection); the utterances of pain are dimmed, only now and again a sound of joy breaks through and softens the silence. All three offices take place before the main ceremonies of the three holy days.

Finally, in the more advanced teaching, show the faithful the wonderful Oriental liturgy of Holy Week. The texts are available.[21] They show the Oriental vision of the redemption which could only make our theology the richer. We should point out the admirable song: "The Blessed Joseph of Arimathea — sung on Good Friday; the unforgettable office of the Myersphores (or bearers of aromatic spices) together with the most ardent and intimate sorrow of the *Trisagion,* a reminder that the sufferings of Jesus are those of the glorious *Logos;* finally the Saturday night office, which in Byzantine piety has always remained the center of the Christian year and is "the most holy of all vigils." The recurring singing of the *Alleluia* places the Paschal mystery in an extraordinary atmosphere of triumphal joy and pathetical sorrow. It is by starting from this point that Byzantine art can be understood.

C. ASCENSION AND PENTECOST

The mystery of the Ascension is the link between Easter and Pentecost. It takes place at the end of a new forty day period, similar to Lent. During these days Christ "tells us of his Kingdom" as Luke says; he makes us understand that salvation is granted, that the Kingdom of God exists, and at the same time he prepares us for the coming of the Church which will make the Kingdom accessible to the world and prepare man for the glorious espousals at the end of all time.

The liturgy of this feast is focused on two points: on the exultation of the Church celebrating the entry of glorified humanity into the bosom of the Trinity (in Jesus the first fruits of the world return into the Father's bosom); and on the expectation of the Spirit who is to come "so that we may not be left orphans,"— the

---

21. F. Mercenier, *La prière des Église de rite byzantin* Vol. II, Chevetogene, 1948, gives the texts of the Oriental Easter.

Lord returns to us in the Holy Spirit. It is a great pity that catechetic teaching about this feast is generally limited to speaking of heaven in a disincarnate manner, and does not mention the cosmic or eschatological aspect of our Lord's going up to heaven. This feast should in fact make us understand that if Christ is to be assimilated by, and clothed with humanity, it is necessary that this incarnation continue, not only in a spiritual sense but also realistically.

In order that the body of Christ may be offered to the Father and communicated to men within time and space, it is in fact necessary that there be men who, through their special consecration and by certain gestures and words act and speak in Christ's stead. The authenticity of the sacramental order depends on this: it is based on the Church which is "Jesus communicated by the Holy Spirit." This communication is the Pentecost.

3. The feast of Pentecost has the same solemnity as Easter; it is in fact one single feast, for it is only after fifty days that the work of Christ was accomplished and became communicable for centuries. The number fifty (seven times seven weeks plus one) symbolizes the entry of the universe into the plenitude of the Kingdom.[22] This is the reason why the eschatological aspect of this feast is so strongly marked in the liturgy; the over-abundance of charismatic gifts of the Spirit, the miracle of the languages, the preaching of the day of the Lord, all this reveals the true sense of this day of Pentecost. The feast of Pentecost is therefore much more than "the feast of the Holy Spirit"; it is the feast of Jesus Christ's espousal with his Church in the Holy Spirit; it is the beginning of the realization of the Kingdom; it is the birth of the real People of God; it is the birth of the Church without which no liturgical mysteries would exist (Easter included),

---

22. J. Danielou, *Lord of History,* Chicago, 1958.

without which Christ could be nothing to us, for he would not have become "our head, our vine and our spouse."

The volume on the Church will make all this clear. Here it suffices to point out that Pentecost is also *the feast of Christ*. The liturgy of the period after Pentecost can be presented as an extension of the catechism on Christ *"who shall remain with us until the end of all centuries."* The feast of Corpus Christi (fairly inexactly popularly termed as the "feast of God"), the feast of the Sacred Heart (to remind us of the incarnate love of God, the center of the work of salvation), the feast of the Apostles Peter and Paul (underlining that the Church rests on these two columns, and especially on the rock which is Peter), that of the Assumption (which manifests the Almightiness of the redemption of Christ in Mary), and finally the feast of All Saints, all resume the liturgical year in the vision of that celestial Jerusalem to return one day, clad like a bride, *whose light is the Lamb*. The key-note of the time after Pentecost is "Christ will return." The prayer of the Church at this time is "Marathana, Come Lord Jesus" which ends the Scripture, as it ends the liturgical year by a vision of the Parousia.

SOME RECENT RESEARCH IN CHRISTOLOGY (1955-65)

1. The distinction made between the two christological traditions has become more marked recently. On the one hand the scheme Word-Flesh, Word-Man, reflects the fundamental problem, namely that of reconciling the immutable transcendency of God with the "becoming" of the Incarnation; on the other there are many trends in the "Antiochian" tradition which require further analysis.

The "Antiochian" tradition can be divided into *two groups*. That of Diodorus of Tarsus, who was less concerned with the soul of Jesus than with reconciling the immutability of God with

the historical fact of Incarnation, chiefly connecting it with the
neo-paganism professed by the Emperor Julian the Apostate. On
the contrary, the trend represented by Theodore of Mopsuestia,
rooted in the tradition of Eustathius of Antioch, was endeavoring
to show the reality of the *human soul* in Jesus. Besides, in both
groups there were some who clung to the "Alexandrian" Word-
Flesh order.

As regards the reality of the *human soul* of Jesus, it is becoming
more and more apparent that the 4th century Fathers saw a
solution in the Origenist school of Didymus the Blind. An erroneous conception of the union of the human with the divine in
Jesus Christ made the Arians attribute passions (such as the
Gospel tells of in the account of Christ's agony) to "Divinity";
from this it followed that the Word was only an inferior and
created divinity, since passion, or a change of any kind was
incompatible with the Divinity. The real answer to this difficulty
about the suffering of Jesus lies in the reality of a *human* soul in
Jesus. Eustathius of Antioch was the first to see this point, but it
seems he was unable to avoid the dangers of dualism. Athanasius
and Cyril, while they affirmed the presence of a human soul in
Jesus, apparently did not see that herein lay the difficulty of
the Arians. At this point Didymian tradition represents a very
important addition. In a still unpublished commentary on the
Psalms (the author is very probably Didymus the Blind) it is
affirmed that the "soul of Jesus is not an immutable *ousia*, since
there is no immutable being besides the Trinity"; and since he
"began to tremble and to be in agony," his soul is not "immutable," because the soul Jesus assumed is other than the "Trinity,"
it naturally felt the pang of agony and horror, in the words of
the Apostle, "despising the happiness offered to him he supported
the cross without regard to the shame." The integrity of his
humanity is therefore well confirmed. Moreover the author of
this commentary emphasizes that Jesus did not know sin. But he
specifies that it was not *in spite of* his human character that this

was so, but *because* of the human integrity of his soul. Indeed it "is because the soul of Jesus has kept the likeness of God that he never knew and never committed sin; it is from this viewpoint that he is said to be Son of Man, that is to say the one who was made in the image and likeness of God." In other words the "soul of Jesus is a wholly human soul, but his consubstantiality with us should not make us forget that he was protected from sin, for his soul was able to fulfill a part which our souls could not." It was therefore because this soul was holy that it could guarantee the absence of sin in Jesus, and *hence* his perfect consubstantiality, sin not being part of the divine image in whose likeness man was created.

The underlying conception here is an Aristotelian and Stoic anthropology. Recent research has underlined the importance of this trend, so that we may now speak of the "Stoicism of the Fathers." [23] Even if the solution offered by the commentator of the Psalms does not assure the perfect impeccability of Jesus as a man (for the doctrine of the soul, faithful to the divine image, only implies what, for want of a better word, we call sinlessness), it offers a solution on which subsequent theology should have been engaged. The very slow disappearance of this tradition regarding the human soul of Jesus (it is no longer found in the Alexandrian tradition) can doubtless be explained by the subsequent condemnations of Origen's ideas by which, however, it was partly inspired.

Finally there is the unpublished work of the late J. Lebon [24]

---

23. The best book to read is by M. Spanneut, *Le stoicisme des Pères de l'Église. De Clement de Rome a Clement d'Alexandrie* (Coll. Patristica Sorbonensia No. 1) Paris, 1957.

24. This is an edition of texts lost in the Greek version, but which exist in a Syrian version by the monk Marcien. While waiting for this publication, entrusted to the care of Professor A. van Roey of the University of Louvain, see J. Lebon's: *Le moine Saint Marcien,* in *Miscellanea Hist. in hon. A. De Mayer,* Louvain, 1946, p. 181-193.

which will perhaps allow us to establish the existence of a *christological tradition* which is both *anti-Apollinarian and anti-dualist* (in its opposition to Theodore of Mopsuestia). This means that there existed in the region of Antioch at the end of the 4th century a trend which used the formula of "one nature," and was therefore very much orientated towards the ontological unity of Christ, and against the errors of Apollinaris (thus safeguarding the necessary distinction between the divine and the human in Jesus).[25]

Recent works elucidate the resurrection as a *Mystery of salvation*. The text in Rom. 1, 2-4: — "The Gospel of God, promised long ago by means of his prophets in the Holy Scriptures, tells us of his Son, descended, in respect of his human birth, from the line of David, but in respect of the sanctified spirit that was his, marked out miraculously as the Son of God by his resurrection from the dead; our Lord Jesus Christ" (quoted from the Knox Bible) underlines the connection between resurrection, the power of the Lord and the power of the Spirit.

P. Benoit has made some decisive research on the *institution of the Eucharist* and the *Ascension*. The outcome is that certainly the breaking of bread is linked in the earliest Christian tradition with the "last supper," but also with the meal Christ took together with his Apostles *after* the resurrection: this reveals the connection between the first Apostolic preaching and the ritual of the Eucharist.[26]

Moreover "when we say and believe with the Church that Christ ascended to heaven in glory where he sitteth at the right hand of the Father," we mean thereby that he entered forever

25. On this point see D. M. Baillie: *God was in Christ*. An Essay on Incarnation and Atonement, London, 1948 (the Anglican viewpoint).

26. P. Benoit, *Exegèse et théologie*, Paris, 1961, Vol. I, pp. 164-262; J. Dupont, *Les pélerins d'Emmaüs* in *Miscellanea biblica B. Ubach* (Coll. *Scripta et documenta*, No. 1, Montserrat, 1953, pp. 349-374).

the new and final spiritual world of which he forms the first particle, a world which is inaccessible through our senses or imagination, but supremely real, far more real than is the actual world. Together with innumerable ancient witnesses of Christianity we like to think that he inaugurated this new world on the day of his resurrection when he was carried away from the tomb by the Spirit, to be exalted at the side of the Father." [27]

It would seem necessary somehow to reverse the usual catechetic viewpoint, for, after all, the first grain of Apostolic catechesis ever to be written down was the fact of the resurrection of Jesus; his discourses and miracles and the account of his childhood were added later in order to explain this fundamental significance.[28]

In this sense the "event," the coming (advent, if the liturgical term is preferred) is fully realized in the resurrection according to Act. 13, 33. "God raised Jesus to life. Thus it is written in the second Psalm. Thou art my son, I have begotten thee in this day." The liturgical and catechetic presentation of the "coming" of God into this world should therefore begin with the resurrection and descend again to the mystery of the terrestrial life of Jesus. It should be a first aim of catechetics to restore the Paschal Feast to the first place, for it must be recalled that the feast of Christmas is still the most popular among Catholic peoples, and that of the three days of Holy Week the essential one, the Paschal vigil, is the least frequented or understood. Before being an event, the Resurrection is an advent; this is surely a logical order since leaving the grave could not be a coming of the Lord

27. P. Benoit, *op. cit.* Vol. I, pp. 363-411; at p. 411 the passage quoted is on p. 411; cf. also in Mt. 27, 52-53 (the dead who rose at the death of Christ) G. Tittonato, *La risurrezione dei Morti*, Mt. 27, 52-53 in *Sapienza* IX (1956) pp. 131-150.

28. F. Neirynck: *L'évangile de Noel* selon Saint Luc, Études religieuses, Liege-Paris, 1960.

in his glory if it were not the same time in a sense, an event, a historical fact, *the* historical fact of the "sacramental" story. This "advent" of the Kingdom is also a victory of Jesus, and in the end of his Church.[29]

After this the *resurrection's significance for salvation* should be better elucidated. An old book by Durwell, which has reappeared in a new edition [30] is still the best study on this subject. The connection between incarnation, death and resurrection, as the pouring out of the Holy Spirit and the effects of the resurrection, namely Jesus Christ Lord, Son of God Almighty, eternal Priest, are presented in a picture with the resurrection, the birth of the Church, her continued life in the resurrected and the progress and the accomplishment of the Paschal mystery within the Church. Catechetics inspired by these ideas offers both a *revelation* and a deliverance to the audience, especially the connection between sin and death; redemption being a total revival, and this is decisive in a "copernican" revolution that should be brought about in the conscience of all Christians. A change from a too juridical and moralizing view of Christian life to a traditional vision, wherein the victory over sin is at the same time a victory over death (both of body and of soul), that is of the entire man, seems the first duty of christological catechetics.[31]

Finally a theological reflection on the "glorious body" is necessary, as much from the point of view of Christ as from that of the final end. K. Rahner has shown the presence of a catechism "not printed, but of the heart" wherein resurrection hardly figures

---

29. J. Comblain, *La résurrection. Essai, Bruxelles-Paris,* 1958 follows this plan.

30. F. X. Durwell, *Resurrection,* New York, 1960.

31. See also P. Bourgy, *La résurrection du Christ et les chrétiens* (Coll. *Études religieuses,* No. 739), Paris, 1959; J. Thomas, *Le résurrection,* Paris, 1959; Y. Congar, *La Péntecôte,* Chartres, Paris, 1956.

at all, whereas it figures in the "printed" example, or to be more precise in the current catechism of the faithful, where among truths which have become *unintelligible,* or almost non-existent, the resurrection is the first to be left out.[32] J. Guitton distinguishes between apparitions to mystics, which have something in common with the apparitions of Jesus, and bodily manifestations to which we are used, which require no "faith" in order to be manifested. Guitton shows that although in themselves the apparitions were not necessary for the founding of the Church, which is founded on the testimony of the Apostles, nevertheless they have a precise purpose, namely, in a world of three dimensions to make visible the presence of a so to speak fourth dimension, which is at the same time historical and transhistorical, i.e. that of an effective and powerful incarnate Word present in the Church. Finally he also insists on the notion of the body.[33]

Regarding this last point, present day phenomenology empha-sizes that the body is both an instrument for acting on the world (thus the "immeasurably enlarged body of humanity" of which Bergson spoke), and the same time a sign of its own presence; we "have" a body but also we "are" a body, not in the sense that we reduce ourselves to material, but meaning that we can never make an abstraction of our precise "situation" in time and space — the "body" then being the mediator of our bodies to others and of the presence of others to ourselves. In the love between husband and wife, for example, the intensification does not mean a progressive disincarnation, but a more and more de-tailed "incarnation where the slightest flutter of an eyelash might mean far more than any explicit statement: the body has become

---

32. K. Rahner, *Schriften zur Theologie,* Vol. II, Cologne, 1955, pp. 211-227.

33. J. Guitton, *Le problème de Jésus,* 2 Vol., Paris, 1952, which con-tains in Vol. II, an analysis of the problem of resurrection. It is taken up again succinctly in *Jésus,* Paris, 1956.

a language wherein there is both the limitation of the individual person and its extension into an inter-subjectivity. Remember that whereas in many texts on the resurrection the word "body" implies the precariousness of the human condition, and "spirit" means power, at the farthest limits, where we speak of the Spirit of God, we mean the very power of God which is identical with his holiness and his glory. Here one can foresee a theology of the "glorious body," where "glory" permits a more multiple presence, one by which human beings can act with more effect upon each other. The Heavens, considered as a communion of the elite in justice and love, appears thus essentially linked with the resurrection of the Lord, whose force is communicated to those bought back through the sacraments. The testimony of the saints, whose life is not "disincarnate," but on the contrary present, acting and multiplied in love and in attention to the details of every life they meet, also elucidates this perspective.[34]

2. The resurrected Christ leads us to the Father. Recent research has accentuated the importance of apophatic, negative theology, considering it one of the essential facts of Christology.[35] Its spiritual doctrine has been renewed [36] as well as the morals which

----

34. A valuable addition to phenomenology is the discovery of the dimension "body"; P. Ricoeur in *Philosophie de la volonté*, Vol. I, *Le volontaire de l'involontaire*, Paris, 1949, pp. 82-124 gives a remarkable analyses. R. Guardini, *Last things*, Notre Dame, 1966, should be read for the reflections on "Kingdom of the end of time."

35. We quote some important works; R. Roques *L'universe Dionysien* (Coll. Theol. No. 29) Paris 1954; H. de Lubac *Exegèse médiévale. Les quatre sens de L'écriture*, 3 Vol. (Coll. Theol. No. 41-42) Paris, 1959-60; J. Meyendorff, *Introduction a l'étude de Gregoire Palamas* (Coll. *Patristica Sorbonestica* No. 3), Paris, 1959, and from the same author *St. Gregoire Palamas et la mystique orthodoxe* (Coll. *Maitres spirituels* No. 20), Paris, 1959; P. Kovalevsky, *St. Serge et la spiritualité russe* (Coll. *Maitres spirituels* No. 16) Paris, 1959.

36. *History of Christian Spirituality,* under publication with the

appear as "the law of Christ." [37]

---

collaboration of J. Bouyer, J. Leclercq, F. Vandenbroucke, L. Cogent (2 vols.), New York, 1964, has this concept; J. F. Six, *L'itinéraire spirituel de Charles de Foucauld*, Paris, 1959; G. Thils, *Christian Holiness*, Tielt, Belgium, 1961.

37. B. Häring, *Law of Christ*, 3 vols. Newman, 1961-66, is about to become a classic. It is needless to point out that for the moment all research on the Dead Sea manuscripts are at an analytical and critical stage: one has become infinitely more prudent in comparison with the New Testament environment and the figure of Jesus; while the comparisons on the former seem certain they are very doubtful regarding the figure of Jesus whose "originality" becomes more and more patently clear. As for the problem of the Jewish people in its relation with the Christians, this question has become common knowledge after the novel by A. Schwarz-Bart, *Le dernier des justes*, Paris, 1959, which is now disturbing Christians. The problem is threefold: there is that of the mystical Jewish traditions and their importance in "classical" Rabbinism; there is that of anti-Semitism, and finally the tragedy of Jewish unbelief in the present century. For what can interest the catechist read: P. Demann, *La catechèse chretienne et le peuple de la Bible*, Paris, 1952. For more complete information read also: A. Chouraqui, *Histoire du judaisme* (Coll. *Que sais-je?* No. 750) Paris, 1957; S. W. Baron, *Histoire d'Israel, Vie Sociale et réligieuse*, 3 Vol. appeared, Paris, 1956-1961, (from its origins to the eve of the expansion of Islam); L. Poliakov, *Histoire de l'antisémitisme*, Vol. I, *Du Christ au Juifs de cour;* Vol. II, *De Mahomet aux Marranes*, Paris, 1955-1961; J. Isaac, *Genèse de l'antisémitisme*, Paris, 1956; G. G. Scholems, *Les grands courants de la mystique juive*, Paris, 1960, P. Demann, *Les Juifs, Foi et Destinée* (Coll. *Je sais, je crois* No. 134), Paris, 1961. As for the Islamic viewpoint on Christ read M. Hayek, *Le Christ de l'Islam*, Paris, 1959.

PART II
MARY

CHAPTER I

THE VIRGIN
IN CONTEMPORARY MENTALITY

THE survey we are proposing is implied by what we have already outlined on the subject of Jesus Christ; but there is also something more here, namely the Church, for Mariology cannot be imagined independently of a twofold relation; on the one hand with Christology, and on the other with ecclesiology. We are here entering a field where literature can give us little help; the mystery of the Virgin has no meaning except within a Christian attitude. Yet it is not as if the wide public had not been aware, even passionately aware, of the definition of the Assumption, for the press has acquired the habit of commenting, sometimes in a fantastic manner, on the principal acts of the Sovereign Pontiff. Moreover the fascination extraordinary apparitions exercise in troubled times has not been missing in the case of the Virgin. However, the interest in papacy is more closely connected with the doctrine of the Church; as for out-of-the-way phenomena, it is not from them that our survey will set out for they must be elucidated theologically. Our subject will above all be doctrinal and sociological.

I. MARY IN THE MINDS OF NON-CHRISTIANS

As for our Savior the reactions of the unbeliever towards Mary can be either negative or positive.

1. THE NEGATIVE ATTITUDE

In the minds of unbelievers the belief in the Virgin Mary appears a mere residue of a childish mythology; man who has arrived at the scientific age must discard it, as an adult discards his childhood's toys. It should here be repeated that this way of judging exists in countless scientific spheres.

A somewhat less radical attitude concedes the legitimacy of a feminine cult in man's religious behavior, but all it sees in the Virgin is a Catholic variant of those fables of goddesses, mothers or daughters of kings who are supposed to have given birth without human intervention. Here we recognize the same syncretism we mentioned in connection with Jesus Christ.

In the same series, but with more detail, some see in the devotion to Mary a form of sentimental inhibition, "a transfer of the sensuality of the chaste," an analogue of the "eternal feminine."

There are other non-believers who see in Mariology one of the means whereby Popes, or priests in general, exercise their power; this conception goes so far as to say that the Church, having revived paganism, has surreptitiously re-introduced into the Gospel message the old idolatry which needs gods (the saints) and goddesses (the Virgin and the female saints).

Huxley's *Perennial Philosophy* expresses this point of view crudely; he says that the great part played by the places of pilgrimage, the Mary statues, are the indication of a kind of white magic which the Church uses in order to maintain her flock. But even if some manifestations do give the impression that super-

stition plays the chief part, needless to say that this is too simple
an approach. The greatest miracle in Lourdes, for example, is
that the pilgrims begin to go to confession and communion; con-
versions from processions at Fatima prove that, even if at times
the appearance is disconcerting; God makes use of it to draw
man up to a *supernatural* plane. The banishing of all external
and popular aspects of religion, is in most cases the result of a
certain pride of the spirit; as Gabriel Marcel says, grace is dealt
out to fit the condition of men, and follows unexpected roads.
"It is a law of all historical works," writes J. Guitton, "to be thus
colored by circumstances, and it is certain that the cult of Mary,
like all things that are frail, is subject to excesses and corruption." [1]
If therefore popular means of devotion have to be used to bring
men to the proper supernatural plane, as happens in fact in the
true devotion to Mary. This is far from being a case for an inhuman and entirely anti-religious purism banishing this very
concrete Marian cult. The paradoxical appearance of religious
awakening at contact with Marian ceremonies is one sign, amongst
many others, of a providential law whereby "God makes use of
things that are not, in order to confound things that are." "He
confounds the wisdom of the wise," says St. Paul. This obviously
does not mean that all popular Marian devotions can be approved;
it would be advisable to point out that the Church forbids many
forms of Marian devotion, e.g. the expression *Virgo sacerdos,*
which is prohibited, together with some iconographic represen-
tations illustrating this expression. We shall return to this later,
but the essential thing is to keep the *hierarchy* of the values
sufficiently apparent.

Finally, and this is at present a wide-spread attitude, there is
the rejection of Marian devotion on the grounds that it is a form
of bourgeoise sentimentality, an unhealthy embodiment of that

---

1. J. Guitton, *La Vierge Marie,* 2nd Ed., Paris, p. 214.

"feminism" whose pre-eminent representative, Nietzsche saw in Rousseau.

We are here thinking of that too general mentality of our century which unduly exalts strength, toughness, and dangerous living. It was not only the totalitarian mystics who were contemptuous of all tenderness, delicacy and femininity in love; authors like Montherlant endeavored to turn woman into the "comrade" of man, in sportive and "virile" occupations as in pleasure. In this line the kind of counter-nature love, such as it appears in modern literature today, is the opposite of all Marian devotion; the part this concept of love played in Nazism is well known; there is an example of it in *Le dernier civil* by Glaeser. Without falling into these aberrations, Marxism, too, bans all "feminine" love and tenderness; by definition the Marxist ideology is masculine; in it woman finds her advantage in the measure she behaves like a man, as for example by fighting in a war. The truth is that the harshness expressed in these words of Malraux "destiny is the business of men, handled by men," is the opposite of a weakness of character. Violence has in our days been built into a system; it is the mark of a civilization which denies womanhood and wants to be purely masculine; it is the source of that jarring oratory which characterizes so many public men of our generation and which it is best to avoid.

From this first survey it should be clear by now that Marian devotion is a complex and a precarious thing. It should never appear as a compromise with elements of that turbid religiosity which still haunts the slumbering primitive in us; it should rather temper the brutality, the vanity and the violence which threaten man. It seems that true Marian devotion should not be formulated "from below," that is to say founded on the psychological needs of man, but "from above," from Revelation itself, so as to come down again to men and activate the delicate synthesis of spontaneous psychology. Despite it having a real value, the working method of those who, without being believers, approve the cult of Mary is wrong in as much as they are too exclusively orientated from the bottom upward.

2. THE POSITIVE ATTITUDE

There are unbelievers who respect in the Virgin "the perfect woman," the ideal which man must contemplate for himself, like an enlarged image of himself, so as to rise to a truly human level. One could for example point to the *double nostalgia* there is in man; for *virginity* and for maternal *fecundity*. These two desires are irreconcilable, since maternity brings with it the loss of virginity, and virginity is sterile, at least in the psychological order. Without believing strictly that Mary was at the same time virgin and mother, these religious philosophers estimate that the Christian "myth" is useful and even indispensable, for it maintains the tension, and the contradiction between the two nostalgias, which are conjointly necessary for the spiritual promotion of man.

Representatives of this tendency will for example underline the part played by courtly love on the development of Marian devotion and vice versa the influence of this devotion on courtly love; they will affirm that the advancement of woman is bound to the spread of Christianity and in it to devotion to Our Lady, in which it is playing a growing part in the West.[2] A. Comte thought that the idea of the Virgin Mother "could become an ideal aim for the purest and the most eminent women and above all give the new religion a synthetic summary, equivalent to what the institution of the Eucharist gave Catholics. He even thought that the utopian idea of a fertile virginity could serve even the most positive biological science by giving it a goal, which is at the same time impossible and desirable, in the same way as the utopia of transmuting metals exalted the pre-scientific

2. For all this read *Le coeur* (Coll. *Études carmélitaines*) Paris, 1951 and our own analysis in *Coll. Mechliniensia* XXII (1952) No. 3.

activities in the Middle Ages." [3] Without going so far, a writer
like Marcel Proust shows an *absurd* immense nostalgia in all
his works for "maternal Purity" and virginity. Massis has a correct
hypothesis on this point; [4] Bergson, too, has said (whereby he
almost fully admitted Catholic truth) that through the Marian
mystery "woman could teach man continency, in the same way
as she had taught him pleasure." [5]

Apologetics can use this argument which belongs in the psychological order, but prudently withal, in order to explain the reason-
ableness of the dogma of the *virginal maternity* of Mary; here the
Virgin is the divine accomplishment of a spiritual need in the
very substance of man, here is his dream of the virginal and
maternal woman, the ideal never attained (only very imperfectly
by some Christian couples), and never realized in the psychological field. But great care should be taken, for this argument
does not prove the dogma as such, and still less is this dogma
true because it expresses this tendency of man (this would be
modernism), but only to say that *revealed* truth could appear
reasonable in a man who observes this twofold nostalgia in himself. Experience has shown us that this attitude has often cleared
the way for access to faith; once this preliminary obstacle is re-
moved, intelligence can better face the examination of historical
reasons which are, as such, the foundation of the reasonable character in the faith in Marian dogma.

We will add that this consideration of the synthesis between
virginity and fecundity, which is achieved in Mary is by nature
such as to prepare the soul for the perception of the mysteries

---

3. Quoted by J. Guitton, *op. cit.*, p. 201, No. 1.

4. Ibid., p. 207, No. 1, and H. Massis, *D'André Gide à Marcel Proust*,
1948. Read for example in *Les plaisirs et le jours*, the called *Violante ou la
mondanité*. Ch. Briand in *Le sécret de Marcel Proust*, absolutely misjudges
the sense of maternal nostalgia in Proust.

5. *Les deux sources de la morale et la réligion*, Paris, 1937, p. 327.

of the divine espousals of God with humanity in the Church, in the soul, in the priesthood, and in the Virgin; everywhere the same truth reappears, the virginal fecundity, for example in our Mother the Church. Moreover in the pansexual and aphrodisiac civilizations of our time, the discovery of psychological implications in Mariology, are of such a nature that they deliver the spirit from its sensuality and to direct it towards an aspect which, for example, helps us to understand that the marriage of Joseph and Mary represents an archetype of Christian marriage.[6]

Another aspect of the same tendency amounts to saying that Marian devotion is necessary to soften and to spiritualize the always somewhat brutal force which marks the behavior of man (if he is masculine); or better still that in the dynamism of the masculine being there is the constant risk of Luciferan pride which is infinitely more pronounced than in women.

We recall the reflections of Peter Wust on women, "the vestals of creation," who must balance the Luciferan pride of man. We have already pointed out in writing on Graham Greene, that his most profound feminine characters are those "angels of pity," who like so many Antigones are all "sisters of mercy" of whom Rimbaud dreamed; that this is a further extension leading to the devotion to the Virgin is obvious.[7] The books of the Christian authoress, Gertrude von Le Fort, especially *La femme éternelle*, give the Catholic aspect of this tendency.

---

6. See at this point A. Frank-Duquesne, *Création et procréation*, Paris, 1951, and *Vie Spirituelle*, June, 1949, devoted to this subject.

7. Concerning all this cf. P. Rostenne, *Graham Greene, témoins des temps tragiques*, Paris, 1950, chapter on women.

II. THE VIRGIN MARY IN JUDAISM AND ISLAM

It seems to us very important to remind the professor of religion that religious Judaism and Islam profess a devotion to Mary which, though not equal to Christian faith, contains some of its elements. It would be desirable if Christians were more conscious of the fact that believing Jews and Moslems are "their brothers," since Abraham was their common ancestor. This aspect would make it easier to understand that in a sense Christians, Moslems and Jews fight on the same spiritual front in the war against every form of atheism; moreover an elucidation of common viewpoints of this tradition would give a better protection to the Christian intelligence against any compromise with the synthetic mysticism or pantheism which threaten us today. It seems to us that one way of making this fundamental connection perceptible for certain Christian aspects, is to point out that both Jews and Moslems have a certain devotion to Mary, the mother of Jesus.[8]

Devout Jews, although they do not admit the Messiah in whom we believe, nevertheless recognize in Mary one of the most perfect incarnations of the *anawim*, the "little ones" whom the Old Testament exalts for their piety, goodness and fervor in their expectation of the Kingdom, in contrast to the bad shepherd who rules with a rod of iron. Whereas in the past Judaism rejected in one block of reprobation Christ together with his mother, a new development has since evolved towards a better understanding of the *facts* that are reported in the Gospels. Many Jewish writers recognize the religious significance of Jesus and Mary; their atti-

---

8. We refer to two sources for further information on the subject, the Review *Cahiers Sinoniens* directed by P. Demann, and the writings of Louis Massignon, extracts of which are to be found in *Dieu vivant*.

tude is similar to that of the Judeo-Christians, of whom we spoke in the chapter on Jesus Christ.

Mary is at the point where the Ancient Law meets the New. The entire significance of her vocation can only be understood if she is viewed *against an Old Testament background;* it is impossible to have a clear understanding of the first chapters of *Matthew* and *Luke* without referring to the biblical environment, and this we have in common with the Israelites.

As for the Islam, the reader should refer to the works of Abd-el-Jalil. The Moslems venerate in "Myriam" the mother of one of the prophets previous to Mahomet, and there exists a true devotion to her; this has been found at least in the oldest parts of the Koran.[9]

III. THE VIRGIN MARY AND NON-CATHOLIC CHRISTIANS

Especially since the publicity given to Protestant and Orthodox reactions to the dogma of the Assumption it is no longer possible to teach Mariology to the faithful without taking account, at least in its main lines, of the reactions of dissident Churches. Through the dogma of the Assumption the structure of all Mariology is questioned in the attacks which were made widely known by the press and diffused into the minds of Catholics. Moreover we like to hope that teachers, catechists and preachers have by now realized that it is no longer possible to present any Christian doctrine without having in mind the main forms it will take in the creeds of dissidents. Theology has nothing to fear from these confrontations, it can but gain from them more depth and a surer balance.[10]

---

9. Abd-el-Jalil, *La dévotion à Marie dans l'Islam* is the chief work on this subject.

10. We think it is useful in teaching catechetics to leave aside the too polemical presentation of truths.

1. THE VIRGIN MARY AND ORTHODOXY

Orthodoxy [11] supplies us with a double paradox. The first can be fairly well expressed thus: on the one hand Orthodox piety gives Mary an eminent position, apparently more important even than in Catholicism, on the other this privileged position of the Mother of God never threatens to overshadow the absolutely central situation of Christ in the work of salvation. Whereas with other Catholics certain developments of Mariology seem at times to endanger the right understanding of the *unique* mediator, Jesus, this danger is entirely absent in Orthodoxy.

The examples of the place Mary takes in Byzantine liturgy are innumerable. We will point out the two following: if the feast of the Annunciation coincides with Good Friday the *liturgy combines the two offices,* for it seems impossible for Orthodoxy to leave out the part played by the Mother of God in the Incarnation; whereas in the Latin office of the *Triduum sacrum* the supression of the doxology and the hymns brings about almost total absence of any mention of the Virgin, the Byzantine ritual constantly associates Mary with the sufferings of her son, e.g. in the admirable office of the *Myrrhophoroi* on the evening of Good Friday, when liturgy brings onto the scene Mary watching by her son's tomb. That breath of fervent emotion which transpires from this liturgy of grief comes partly from the constant presence of the Mother of God. She participates in the whole tragedy, not only as a historical person, but mysteriously representing the Church and all believers in the drama of salvation. The passionate force which inspires the liturgy of Holy Week is deeply rooted in this virginal

---

11. Here we are taking Orthodox in its ancient tradition, not in the form it has taken in its slavophile movement or for example in the sophiology of Boulgakov.

compassion of the Mother of the Savior, for in the Church Mary does not stand for a passive, but, for a dynamic element.[12]

All who practice Byzantine liturgy know that the Acathist hymn addressed to Mary who "is greater than the Cherubim" keeps recurring; they know that Mary's presence in no way lessens the radiance of the glorified Christ, the *Pantocratôr*.

The explanation of this paradox lies in the fact that Mary is constantly seen in the light of the Resurrection of Christ; she is herself closely linked with his Incarnation. The Annunciation connects the Virgin to Christ and his work of restoring the plenitude of Adam in the Resurrection, the crowning of the Passion of God.[13]

The second paradox in Orthodox Mariology is that it roots the Virgin in our humanity while at the same time it associates her with the principle of Salvation, that is to say Christ. On the one hand Mary seems filled with the most gentle and radiant humanity, on the other she appears in the transcendent order of salvation, associated with the New Adam. In the liturgy of the Eastern Church the humility of her human appearance in the Gospel is thus joined with the exaltation of the Mother of God.

In the words of Theophanos "the exceptional grace of which Mary has been the recipient has not broken our relationship with her. The liturgical office of the Church mentions her father and mother, in order to show that the glory of Mary has not deprived her of humanity, and that this glory is destined for all of us. The elements of her terrestrial life — her birth, her holiness, which was still an Old Testament saintliness, were so to speak 'condensed in her' until 'at the fullness of time' her consecration

---

12. We have borrowed this explanation from an unpublished exposition by a Greek Orthodox made at a recent Ecumenical meeting. This witness, even added, "Mary is necessary to the divine family."

13. The link between the *Theotokos* and the mystery of Incarnation has a central place in the East.

to God on the day of the Annunciation, her motherhood, the mission of the beloved disciple on her behalf — all these events made up the life of a woman the same as ourselves but who deserved the wonders by which God gratified her. She rejoiced in God, her *Savior*, and *found grace* before God by her purity. She realized in herself the gift of Pentecost, and accomplishes her mission at her Son's throne, anticipating the divinely beautiful glory of all the saints of the Church and resplendent with divine miracles." [14]

The explanation of the second paradox surely lies in the special conception the East has of the first Adam, transfigured by the glory of the divine image. Mary who was the first to incarnate this holiness as an associate and new Eve at the side of the New Adam, also incarnates "human nature" according to the will of God. We refer here to what has earlier been said about Orthodox Christology.[15]

The glory of Mary does not overshadow that of Jesus, the unique mediator, nor does it contrast with the humble conditions of the girl from Nazareth. Orthodox Mariology, as we have so far outlined it, contains nothing whatever contrary to the Latin Mariology of the West. It should also be remembered that Catholic Mariology has two sources, Latin and Oriental. "Whatever problems may arise in their reconciliation, the Roman Church claims for herself all the dogmatic and religious inheritance, from the Greek and Latin Fathers, and from Byzantine and Latin liturgy.... There should in principle be no occasion for discord between the East and the West, all that the Orthodox accept as authority is in fact authority for the Catholics." [16]

Hence here follows this fundamentally important conclusion:

---

14. *Dieu vivant*, No. 18, 1951, p. 97 by Th. Spasky.

15. P. Evdokimov, *L'Orthodoxie*, Neuchâtel, 1959, pp. 148-151.

16. L. Bouyer, *Le culte de la Mère de Dieu dans l'église catholique*, in Irénikon XXII (1949), p. 140; *Le trône de la Sagesse*, Paris, 1957.

the Western theologian is wrong if he ignores Oriental tradition; by examining it as closely as possible he can only find in it the roots of a harmonious cohesion, the key to a theological equilibrium, which might at times appear somewhat fragile in a too exclusively Western-inspired theology. In other words the danger to which sometimes Latin Mariologists seem prone, to exalt Mary to a degree which eclipses the role of the unique mediator, can easily be avoided by the theologian who draws his knowledge from *both* traditions. The ecumenical problems are here again useful in maintaining the internal balance of Mariology.

We refer here to L. Bouyer, who says that Catholic Latin *liturgy* constantly draws from Greek and Oriental sources, at any rate for the feasts of Circumcision, the Nativity of the Virgin, Assumption (at least for the old texts) and Annunciation. It is regrettable that teachers, preachers and theologians do not sufficiently use these texts of the Marian liturgy, for in them they would find a very well-balanced picture of the respective parts played by Christ and by Mary.[17]

However it should be noted that since the Schism, and especially since the 16th century, there has been a certain rigidity in Eastern Marian theology.

The polemical spirit, resulting from the separation, made some of the Eastern theologians refuse the Immaculate Conception, at least in the Western form, and to quibble on difference of faith regarding the recent Western definition of the Assumption.

Faith in the absolute Virginity of Mary has always existed and was never questioned in the East. The different conception of the Greek Fathers of original sin (they prefer the technical name "sin" for the failings of the individual) explains why they did not see in the holiness of Mary an exception, or an exemption of a general "law," but rather underlined the *positive* aspect of Mary's

---

17. L. Bouyer, *Le culte* ... pp. 141 and 153.

initial holiness which, while rooted in the Adamic human race is, together with Christ, the point of departure of salvation. According to Cabasilas, Mary is the ideal type for humanity. It is all the more surprising to see that contact with the West which showed the East the Western reserve regarding the Immaculate Conception, caused a certain shock and brought about a stiffening of the doctrine. It can be explained by the defiance of the acts of Roman primacy which were too polemical in nature in many writings. One will even find in some a certain confusion between Immaculate Conception and virginal conception.[18]

On the subject of the Assumption all Orthodox Churches are one in saying that their Church professes this Christian belief. The reaction of Orthodoxy was to emphasize that they stood equally far from the left extreme, i.e. the Protestants, and the right, attributed to Roman Catholicism. The Orthodox regard the 1950 definition as inopportune, for in their opinion, only an Ecumenical Council could have established it. Moreover, they reject all considerations in the Bull of Promulgation which attach the Assumption to the "privilege" of Immaculate Conception, since they link the "Dormition" exclusively with the Resurrection of the Savior.[19] Through her Assumption Mary presides, together with her Son, over the destinies of the Church; she intercedes, she is the eschatological picture of the Church. Finally the theologians emphasize their belief in the corporal death of Mary which they see more or less implicitly denied by the Bull *Munificentis-*

----

18. This is the content of M. Jugie's *L'Immaculate Conception dans l'Écriture Saints et la tradition orientale* (Coll. *Bibl. Immac.* No. 3), Rome, 1952.

19. It is well to remember that this connection between the Immaculate Conception and the Assumption is noted in the "considerings" of the Bull *Munificentissimus;* these are not guaranteed by infallibility and should therefore not cause any difficulty to our Orthodox brothers.

simus.[20] What therefore Orthodoxy would like is to assure the link between Mary's holiness and the resurrection of Christ, and it refutes what it calls a shift through the "privileges" of the Immaculate Conception.[21]

It should be specified that Greek Orthodoxy has taken a more radical line; besides having clearly affirmed the inopportunity of the 1950 definition, some theologians, it appears, do not even admit that the faith of their Church *has the same object* as the Roman Church. The "Dormition" celebrated on August 15th, would only mean the total union of the *soul* of Mary with her divine Son, nothing positive being said about the state of her *body;* but in that fact Greek Orthodoxy admits the tradition of John of Damascus on the *bodily* Assumption and so there appears to be a certain difficulty.[22]

This slightest reaction towards rigidity in Orthodoxy, chiefly Greek Orthodoxy, has really no effect on the essential point. Were it not for the traditional grievances of the East against the Pontifical authority, and what they consider an abuse of "scholastic definitions," the union of Orthodoxy and Catholicism in Mariology could in principle be easily achieved. While keeping in mind the polemical distortions, here is a treasure the catechist can make good use of in his teaching.

---

20. This is an erroneous interpretation; this point discussion has remained fully free; the Bull is composed in a form which allows for both opinions. Jugie's thesis, that Mary did not die, is far from being current in Catholic Mariology.

21. All this in *Dieu vivant*, No. 18, 1951, pp. 95-96 and *Vers l'unité chrétienne*, No. 28, Dec. 1950, pp. 17-18, article by C. Dumont to whom we owe much. L. Bouyer, *art. cit.*, pp. 151, 156 demonstrates that the "privilege" does not separate Mary from humanity, but is the first realization of salvation.

22. All this is to be found in *Irénikon*, XXIV (1951) pp. 79 and 86-90 by P. Dumont who gives the best balanced picture of Greek Orthodoxy.

2. MARY IN ANGLICANISM

As always, the position of Anglicanism is complex. Regarding the 1950 definition, the official authorities have said that the Anglican Church venerates the Mother of God, since she accepts the first four Ecumenical Councils (therefore that of Ephesus in 431 which defines the virgin maternity of Mary). The Archbishops of York and Canterbury who, as is well known, represent the most official authority of the Church of England, in a sensational declaration affirmed that their Church could not accept as a dogma of faith, necessary for salvation, the bodily Assumption since this is not contained in Scripture or the teaching of the primitive Church.[23] Other, authoritative theologians have, however, shown a more lenient attitude in this subject. The theologian Mascall affirms, for example that both in the Churches of the East and the West faith in the Assumption is a certain *fact* which theological common sense forces us to admit. He specifies that he himself, as well as the Bishop of Exeter (Dr. Mortimer) admits the Assumption for "such a belief, professed almost unanimously ever since the 8th century, can hardly be rejected as false *by anyone who believes that the Church is under the guidance of the Holy Spirit.*" He adds that Mary "has attained the final destiny of the Christians, which is to reign with Christ in glory. She has passed beyond death, beyond the Resurrection and beyond the Last Judgment. She participates in the glory of Christ, she is at his side, she is associated with his eternal intercession. She is already, before the end of time, where we hope to be in the end. She is, so to speak, the triumphant Church, by anticipation in all her holiness, which has by grace been perfectly incorporated in the human nature of the Son of Man. Her entry into

---

23. *Vers l'unité chrétienne*, No. 28, Dec. 1950, p. 16 and *Irénikon*, XXIII (1950) p. 422 sv.

this final state of perfection is described by the word Assumption, it is her entry with her resurrected body into celestial glory." [24]

It is all the more interesting to find that this agreement on the fonts of the doctrine is coupled by Mascall with a rejection of the dogmatic definition *as such*. These two reasons he gives should hold the attention of the theologians. The first is that it is impossible to affirm that faith in this dogma is necessary for salvation when for centuries it has not been clearly known. In defining it the Church has put it on a different level; in ancient ecclesial tradition a definition was made by the Magisterium whenever salvation was *in danger* because of threatening heresies; it was then important to make a definition and impose it under pain of damnation. Since no danger of heresy was manifested in regard to the Assumption, this doctrine has only become necessary for salvation because the Church defined it as such. The second reason amounts to saying that in the act of Nov. 1950 there is a reversal of theological method. The abuse of the term "implicit revelation" according to the author would bring with it this reversal: formerly the Church would have inferred — from the deposit of faith its definition: now one would infer from the presence of this truth in the faith of the Church to its presence in the deposit of revealed truths.[25]

The attitude of the confraternity of Saint Alban, which specializes in dialogue between Anglicanism and Orthodoxy, is also

---

24. This text is by Dr. Mortimer, Bishop of Exeter quoted by Mascall in *Dieu vivant*, No. 18, 1951, pp. 100-101. It is remarkable to see the accord of a fraction of Anglicanism with Orthodoxy and Catholicism on this doctrine of Mary "Eschatological icon of the Church." This latter expression is by L. Bouyer, *art. cit.*, p. 156. Note too that Mascall bases himself upon *Church tradition*. Here the ways part between Orthodoxy, Catholicism, Anglicanism (at least a fraction of it), and Protestant reform.

25. All this in *Dieu vivant*, art. cit., pp. 102-103. In the same issue Y. Congar answered this apparently double but in reality, single argument. Cf. *Tradition et ecuménisme in Irénikon*, XXV, (1952), pp. 364-370.

very interesting; the Roman definition represents one of those mysterious paradoxes of ecumenism; a line of thought hitherto followed must be suddenly broken, only to make place for another, more profound and essential line of research. If the dialogue with the East seems to be interrupted by the gesture of Pius XII, this would only show that ecumenism did not progress along a straight line, but along one that is constantly and providentially broken; this time the line to be discovered is a more profound knowledge of the dogma of the communion of Saints, that is to say the dogma of the *Church,* the Mystical Body, common to the Orthodox, the Catholics, and a fraction of Anglicanism.[26]

Finally it should be added that according to some Anglican thinkers the definition of the Assumption should invite the High Church men to abandon the dialogue with Rome in order to take up again a dialogue with Orthodoxy which they had intended to interrupt.[27]

It appears that the difficulties of Anglicanism in face of the November 1950 definition can be traced to two sources: under the influence of European reform the reason of the Low Church's non-acceptance meets the Protestant attitude which will be discussed later; in the High Church and in anglo-Catholicism, the basis of the dogma is admitted but its "definition" is rejected; here the influence of Orthodox problematics is apparent; here even a crisis can be diagnosed in the dialogue between Catholicism and High Church, a crisis which causes the latter to turn towards the Orthodox world.

---

26. *Vers l'unité chrétienne,* No. 28, Dec. 1950, p. 27. This remark is as correct as profound, for present-day theology orientates towards ecclesiology, as we shall show later.

27. *Irénikon,* XXXIII (1950) p. 423 and cont.

3. MARY IN THE REFORMED CHURCHES

European Protestantism has nowadays once more to fight on *two fronts,* against "Romanizing infiltrations" on the one hand, and against what one calls "Anabaptism" on the other. A recent leading article gave the alarm on the subject of the infiltration of Bultmann's theological modernism; a novel which seems to be a companion to *Journal d'un curé de campagne* shows how strongly theological modernism has influenced some pastors.[28]

This modernism, or if you like this new theological liberalism, is an easy prey to the Nestorian error, and this brings about a minimization of the divine maternity and the virgin conception.[29]

Orthodox Protestantism accepts the Council of Chalcedon with its corollary of Mary's divine maternity: "for them, as for us (at least in principle) Mary is the virgin mother of Jesus according to the flesh." By rejecting ulterior dogmatic developments, Orthodox Protestantism affirms two things, namely that Mary is *within the limits of the Church;* moreover she has such a place therein that she can be called *one of the figures of the Church.* Nevertheless she remains entirely on the other side from Protestantism.

It should be kept in mind that for the Reformation the Church means the assembly of believers, it is constituted by the faith

---

28. No. 21 of *Verbum Caro* the Neo-Calvinist review, published in 1952 points to the growing influence of Bultmann. In No. 22 of the same periodical, R. Stauffer reviews *La Flamme et le vent,* by H. Hatzfeld, Paris, 1952. In it the critic emphasizes that Hatzfeld's opinion should not be considered as the general opinion in Calvinism. Let us add that in a general way a great part of Protestantism defies the MRA (moral rearmament) wherein it sees a sort of "religion of the spirit" which has no place in the Protestant Reformation.

29. H. Hatzfeld, *op. cit.,* pp. 51-56. This opinion should not eclipse the deep human and pastoral value of this book.

in the Word, the essential content of which is God's pardon in Jesus Christ. Keeping this specification in mind, the first point can be illustrated by the words of pastor Thurian: "Reformed theology wants to maintain Mary within the Church; it accuses Catholicism of putting her outside the Church by placing her above and opposite the Church. If Mary marches at the head of those who believed she now marches *with them* and together with them towards her Son, from whom with them she looks for the redemption of her body and eternal glory, having, as they, obtained the remission of her sins, justice and sanctification." Moreover Mary, figures in the Church because she is perfectly believing and directly obedient to the Savior. There can be no question of admitting Mary's spiritual maternity of the Church, or to attribute her a soteriological part. Pastor Roux says, "there is no second Eve, there is only a second Adam." Mary is the exemplary witness of the Church; she is what the Church herself is called upon to be, the one full of grace, the object of God's benediction because of Jesus Christ, the only one who corresponds perfectly with the Word by obedience through faith.

The ideas this position implies are well known; they do not see Mary otherwise than in the light of Christology, as one of its auxiliary prepositions. Whereas, Catholicism would see in Mary a separate consideration. In the case of a gift of God it is an insisting on God the giver, rather than on the gift itself, thereby not seeing that unless God gives *something* He is not really a giver, in other words, to deny human cooperation with God through the grace of God for the realization of salvation; it is also a too extrinsic notion of grace, as much with regard to Mary as the Church; and finally it is a theological method based on a literalizing exploitation of the data of Scripture.[30]

---

30. Y. Congar, *Vers l'unité chrétienne*, No. 48, Dec. 1952, pp. 4-5.
31. *Vers l'unité chrétienne*, No. 28, Dec. 1950, p. 10 and *Rev. Sc. phil. theol.*, 1951, No. 4, p. 621.

However it is important to point out that there is a more radical opposition to Mariology in Calvinism than in Lutheranism.[31] But besides this general tendency there are also more positive tendencies in the present day Reformed Churches.

In 1951, the Lutheran theologian, Asmussen, published a remarkable little book on *Mary Mother of God,* in which he concludes that there is a certain Marian "mediation," not "at the side," of Christ's mediation but "within it." In the same book the author also writes about the truly *sacerdotal* and mediative elements in Lutheran pastoralism.[32] A recent historian has written the history of the cult of Mary in the Lutheran Reform. In it he emphasizes the role of the medieval element in Luther's piety for the Virgin. Moreover he shows that three hundred years were needed to arrive at the totally negative attitude now being attributed to the Reformed Churches, and that in the literature of the past century the Marian theme was more abundant than ever before in German Protestantism. Finally he shows that the 1950 definition provides an opportunity for fruitful work within the Churches and between them.[33]

In Calvinism too, a certain return to Marian devotion is noticeable, especially in the neo-Calvinist group.[34] Pastor Jean de Saussure, in a remarkable meditation, comes very close to the

---

32. The title of the book is *Maria, die Mutter Gottes,* Stuttgart, 1951, reviewed by R. Laurentin, *Iconographie Mariale* in *Vie Spirituelle,* May, 1952, p. 152, pp. 531-532 and Y. Congar in *Vers l'Unité chrétienne,* No. 48, Dec. 1952, p. 6 and *Rev. Sc. phil. theol.,* 1951, No. 4, p. 621 and cont.

33. R. Schimmelpfennig, *Die Geschichte der Marienverehrung im deutschem Protestantismus,* Paderborn, 1952.

34. This group is founded on the Calvinist Congress of 1936. Its founder is Lecerf, its exegete Leenhart; J. L. Leuba and Max Thurian with Pastor Jean de Saussure are its theologians. Read for example J. de Saussure, *Catholicisme réformé,* in *Verbum Caro,* No. 21, (1952), pp. 3-12. (This review is the publisher for this school.)

idea of the Virgin's maternal aspect.[35] Pastor Thurian, firm in opposition to Catholicism, points to the danger of minimizing texts on Mary in Scripture.[36] Finally, F. Quievreux, using the method of exegetes which is based on "numbers," discovered the doctrine of Mary's spiritual maternity in the Gospel of John, thus arriving at the same conclusion, though by different ways, as F. M. Braun in his recent book on the Virgin in St. John.[37]

These tendencies should not prevent us from forgetting the frank opposition of the Reformed Churches to the definition of the Assumption; it is directed as much against the theological method implied by the act of November 1950, as against the contents of the dogma itself.[38] The causes of this opposition of the Reformed Churches are firstly the absence of this belief in Scripture and ancient tradition, and secondly the doctrine of the infallible Magisterium implied in the definition. Moreover they have all solemnly declared that by acting thus the Church has deepened the gulf between the Christian confessions, and expressed their anxiety for the future of the ecumenical movement.[39] As for the context of the dogma itself and Catholic Mariology in general, several Calvinist theologians spoke of a latent Monophysite influence in the Roman Church.[40]

---

35. *Vers l'unité chrétienne*, No. 48, Dec. 1952, pp. 5-6.

36. J. Guitton, *op. cit.*, p. 220, No. 1, quotes a passage written in this sense by Pastor Thurian.

37. F. Quevreux, *La maternité spirituelle de la Mère de Jésus dans l'Évangile de Saint Jean* in *Verbum Caro*, No. 21 (1952), pp. 15-38, reprinted in *Documents de la Vie Spirituelle* (1952), has points of contact with F. M. Braun, *La mère des fidèles, Essais de théologie Johannique* (Coll. *Cahiers de l'actualite religieuse*), Paris, Tournai, 1952.

38. Y. Congar, in *Rev. Sc. phil. theol.*, No. 4, 1951, p. 622.

39. Since then these fears have proved unjustified.

40. For a complete survey of the Protestant attitude, see *Vers l'unité chrétienne*, No. 28, Dec. 1950, pp. 10-16. Regarding the charge of Monophysitism see above all Y. Congar, *Le Christ, Marie et l'Église*, Paris, 1952,

In the following chapter we will return to the Protestant objection on the grounds that there is no mention of the Assumption in ancient tradition; here it will suffice to recall that the standard of Catholic faith is based on the *living* Magisterium, which in virtue of a promise of spiritual assistance has authority to interpret the meaning of the Bible, and the truths contained in the deposits.[41] The Protestant concern about the possibility of a whole series of Marian definitions issuing from the November 1950 definition has been correctly evaluated in the following: "It should be recognized that theologians have been at work in the bosom of the Roman Church in order to reach a similar definition. But there are others, in no smaller numbers, who clearly stand opposed to any ulterior development of Marian theology in this sense. There is no place here to deal with these. We must admit that from the point of view which causes the fear of our Protestant brothers the expressions 'mediator' and 'co-

---

pp. 80-88, and *Rev. Sc. phil. theol.* No. 4, 1951, p. 623, J. L. Leuba, *Verbum Caro,* No. 20, (1950) also points out that Christology is the basis of all discussion on Mariology and ecclesiology. (Cf. *Vers l'unité chrétienne,* No. 38, Dec. 1951, pp. 10-11.) There is also an excellent restatement in *Irénikon,* XXIV, (1951), pp. 390-399. (signed D.L.B.)

41. The best work at present which tries to answer the Protestant arguments is by Fr. Philippe de la Trinité, *Certitude de l'Assumption in Magie des extrèmes* (Coll. *Études Carmelitaines*), Paris, 1952, very competently reviewed by J. Coppens in *Eph. theol. Lov.,* Sept. 1952, pp. 616-619. The author bases his arguments on three principles; the existence of ecclesiastical tradition; the reasons of extreme convenience which almost reach certainty and lie within Scripture logic: and the only qualified intervention being that of the Magisterium. In other words the author adopts the full meaning of the Scriptures which alone the Magisterium can authenticate or discover. The field of historical *promulgation,* he explains, should not be confounded with the *metaphysical* penetration (in our opinion this term is wrongly chosen) of the same truths. History is not only history when it is a case of historical facts which must also be qualified as dogmatic facts. The historical fact is only guaranteed indirectly by the dogma. The

redemptor' are about as unfortunate as could be, and may well justify their fear. But let us add quickly that even if these expressions were to remain, they would be carefully specified, so that the parts played by Mary or her Son could not be confused in the economy of the Redemption. There would be more than a mere differentiation in shade which could not escape the notice of the ordinary faithful, not to speak of experienced theologians." [42]

From this brief survey it is clear that all the Anglican and Protestant difficulties arise from two sources: one is their suspicion of Catholic "Monophysitism"; derived in its final analysis from their incomprehension of Christology; and the other is their ecclesiological conception, differing from ours. The first source takes us back to the chapter on Jesus Christ in contemporary mentality; the second will carry us to the volume on the Church. What seems important here is that the ecumenical problems of Mariology reveal to us that it is the point at which Christology

---

plenary "meaning" is willed by God who is the author of Scripture. The Bible is the intentional mirror of God's loving wisdom, to whom in consequence the power belongs to make the Magisterium declare with full objectivity what he said and intended to say (pp. 181-182). So whereas it is useless to look for explicit Bible passages pointing to the Assumption, or else to use apocryphal "legends," in the following terms: the logic of Scripture, the doctrine consonant with the Bible and situated in its extension which is a necessary consequence of truths explicitly revealed in Scripture. In one word the full sense is that the doctrine (in this case the Assumption) is implied for different reasons in texts which are inspired. It is important to see that so critical an exegete as J. Coppens has rallied to this manner of regarding the Assumption as a "plenary sense" of the Bible in its great themes according to their connections. See also *Irénikon* XXV (1952), p. 369 and Y. Congar, in *Dieu vivant*, No. 18, (1951), pp. 107-112 (for the analogy of faith this author makes use of similar methods to those of the article in *Études Carmelitaines*).

42. *Vers l'unité chrétienne*, No. 28, Dec. 1950, pp. 12-13.

and Ecclesiology meet; in the words of J. Guitton, "Mariology lies at the point of contact between Catholic truths." [43]

A passage by Jean de Saussure in *Contemplation de la Croix*, from which we borrow a quotation used by M. Villain, can tell us much about the vision of a Protestant contemplating in Mary one who is "rich in her sole poverty, great in her sole humility"; it will be noted how this subject is interlaced with that of the Church. As in the original quotation by M. Villain, we too italicize all passages borrowed from or inspired by the Bible. "Poverty of Thy mother, the only richness of the Church. Yes, the one who conceived Thee *only through the power of the Almighty*, and could only follow Thee as far as the foot of the Cross, by sacrificing everything to Thee has remained the type of the virgin soul of all human thought and resource, and lives only by the supernatural work of Thy Spirit in her. She is the model of the *clean of heart*, purified of all that does not come from Thee, whom Thou hast declared happy for *they shall see God*. She is the patron of all who have to shed all the goods of this earth, the vain illusions of philosophy, human traditions and what is wrongly called science and the passions of every kind, or the projects of their hearts, so as to subsist only by Thy grace. She is the image of Thy *poor* whom Thou proclaimed *blessed for theirs is the Kingdom of heaven*. And indeed, whenever the Church was seduced like Eve, and her thoughts were turned away from the simplicity Thou demandest, every time she yielded to the temptation of false riches, and thought she could say: I have

---

43. J. Guitton, *op. cit.*, p. 214. One will find in J. W. Saatman, *Le protestantisme americain*, Louvain, 1953, a review of the situation in the New World; it contains implications regarding Mariology. It should be pointed out that Lutheranism too is undergoing reorganization, not only ecclesiastically but also doctrinally. Cf. the Sept.-Dec. issues of *Vers l'unité chrétienne*. Perhaps Lutheranism too is about to become a "bridge Church," the part Anglicanism has for some time played.

grown rich, I have need of nothing, its weight dragged her to ruin and perdition. Never can she be saved but according to the example of the Virgin; she will remain like her, *blessed* only by conforming to her semblance. Whenever she became worldly and thereby turned the world away from Thee, it was always by repeating with Mary the words, *let it be according to Thy word* whatever the cost, and exposing herself to lose all, to live by the Word alone, that without human help she once again became the mother of innumerable faithful in as many supernatural births. . . . Humility of Thy mother, the only guardian of the Church. . . . Yes, the holy Virgin who always *lowers* herself to make Thee *grow,* remains a better inspiration for Thy Church than what minds which unceasingly magnify Thee and her can imagine. For the Church, too, the real majesty is not to rule, but to serve. And the only way to *glorify herself* is by *glorifying herself in Thee, Lord first.* Therefore those who exalt her for herself do her a double wrong: first they harm *the Church, which is but Thy body* so that this can only be done by hurting Thee; for to deny Thee injures that of which Thou art *the head.* Moreover, whether one wills or not, to give her a separate value from Thee would lower her to the level of this world, for outside of Thee there is only her. No, decidedly, it is only *beside Thy cross,* prostrate at Thy feet and eclipsed by Thy splendor, that the Church can preserve her greatness and divine mission." [44]

IV. MARY IN THE CATHOLIC FAITH

It has been said repeatedly that the 20th century will be a "Marian century." This aphorism should be made explicit, for

---

44. Quoted by M. Villain in *Introduction a l'ecuménisme* (Coll. *Église vivant*), 3rd ed., Tournai-Paris, 1961, pp. 100-101. The reader will have made the necessary adjustments for the Catholic vision of the Church.

as it stands it could lead to misunderstanding, not only amongst
our Reformed brothers, but even among Catholics. If by the term
"Marian century" is meant that an almost exclusive importance
is given to Mariology, because all other theological treatises
having been perfectly clarified and can now be put aside naturally
we cannot agree. It is above all important that Mariology should
not develop so concentrically, so "enclosed within itself" that its
connection with the entity of other Catholic truths should too
often be taken for granted, or difficult to explain. On the other
hand, it is correct to say that this century, as was the last, is rich
in Marian research and discovery; the attention of theologians
has been attracted by certain points which have hitherto remained implicit in Catholic truths. One should approve of this,
provided the Mariologist does not work within abstract deduc-
tions, setting out from a principle (*potuit ... decuit ... fecit*); [45]
but on the contrary contributes in showing "the connections between revealed mysteries among themselves, and their harmony
with the ultimate end of men." [46] We have said above that the
ecumenical problems in Mariology have revealed this key situation;
it is desirable that the expression, "Marian century" should make
room for the well known words of Romano Guardini: "A religious
event of immense consequence is about to be accomplished: the
Church is aware of an awakening in souls." [47] It therefore seems
to us more correct to say that the 20th century is an "ecclesial
century" rather than to say it is a "Marian century," even if
both statements in the end mean the same, though seen from
different angles.

Catholic Mariology should penetrate into the knowledge of

---

45. Y. Congar, in *Dieu vivant*, No. 18 (1951), pp. 100-110.

46. We call attention to the fact that this is the definition of speculative
theology according to the Vatican Council.

47. Quoted by R. Aubert in *Coll. Mechlin*, XVI (1946), p. 27. The
annexed commentary should also be read.

theology more deeply, and theology should make Marian doctrines more comprehensible. It appears that piety and doctrine
can err in two ways, both by too little and by too much.

1. THE ERROR OF THE TOO LITTLE

We are here reproving the tendency to speak too little of the
Virgin Mary, not because we unconditionally accept the *de Maria
nunquam satis*, but because some theologians err through an
exaggerated fear of the development Mariology might take. They
would like to put a stop to the movement and the idea of Marian
piety, not always because of a misplaced fear of archeologism,
but sometimes because of a certain lack of a deeper understanding
of the significance of Marian dogma.[48]

It is important to specify that this attitude is legitimate in face
of such excess as we shall later point out, and which seem alarm-
ing, at least in their immediate appearance. The fact is that these
theologians fear a Mariology which is separated from the body
of theology. On the other hand to exaggerate this fear is not
without danger either. It is for example obvious that it was not
liturgy proper, but what we should term as "liturgism," that led
certain theologians to a too negative attitude in this subject. The
Encyclical *Mediator Dei* on liturgy clearly shows that there are
two tendencies in theology and spirituality, which only too often
clash, instead of joining as they should in *mutual* respect; on the
one hand there is the spirituality based on liturgy and interpreted
in its integral sense; it is suspicious of the countless modern
"devotions" (among which are the devotions to the Virgin), or

---

48. We ask the reader not to misunderstand what we have said and are
further going to say, and not to think that we have in mind any special
theologian. It is rather a question of general tendencies than of explicit
statements. It will be the same concerning the error by excess. In *De Maria
nunquam satis*, cf. *Rev. Sc. phil. theol.*, 1951, No. 4, p. 616.

sees what Heiler calls *Vulgärkatholizismus,* or what Newman described when he said, "the success of a devotion is not necessarily the index of its whole theological truth"; on the other there is the tendency of those who, because they see the weaknesses in an unpopular liturgy or its lack of meaning for the modern man, turn the major part of their apostolic activities towards liturgies which are said to be "modern." [49] It should be added that the vocabulary the partisans of this second trend use is not always fortunate because its biblical, patristic, and liturgic implications are not clear.

The Encyclical offers elements for a synthesis, for having defined liturgy it adds that modern devotion is useful and necessary on condition that "born out of liturgy it shall take us back to it." It is to be regretted that too many Christian polemicists use the Pontifical text indiscriminately, some stress the first part of the Encyclical, in order to condemn the second; the other trend quotes the second part on devotion trying thereby to refute the primacy of the first given to liturgy. It is clear that the defenders of the first ideas are more in line with the Roman document than those of the second, since the liturgy is one of the privileged domains of the ordinary Magisterium of the Church; but it is also no less clear that some "liturgists" exaggerate in their mistrust of Mariology, which might result in their including, along with other aspects to be vigorously denounced, some essential aspects, perhaps badly expressed by the Mariologists who have helped to bring them into the light. It is permissible to ask both parties here for a little more "Catholic sense," that is to say a better understanding of that tradition which, as well as being a resource gained from the past, is also a resource for the past, *gained from the present?* [50] It should as a matter of fact be added that the

---

49. *Quest. Lit. Par.* XXXIII (1952), pp. 219-221.

50. A sort of translation should be made into "traditional, patristic, and scripture language" of this fairly vague vocabulary used by spirituals who

defenders of *Vulgärkatholizismus* stand on the margin of that true Mariology which will be described in its broad outlines elsewhere; far from separating from the traditional past, it returns to it and brings Mariology into the light in its *ecclesiological, christological and eschatological* meaning.

2. Error by Excess

An eminent theologian gave us the main idea: "There are, he said, two ways of thinking theologically on the Blessed Virgin. The one, only too frequent, proceeds schematically in the following manner. It being once and for all established (these theologians would otherwise never touch a given fact) that Mary is the mother of Jesus, the incarnate Word, and that as such she has exceptional "privileges," this theology considers her in herself, and works out a sort of metaphysics or gnosis, for her; a method of deducting from timeless attributes which issue unhampered from these consequences, somewhat as in the treatise on God, His attributes are deduced from the principle of His absolute perfection. However, principles are used here which could be argued, such as: "Mary has by grace all that which God has by nature" (and which is compatible with the condition of a creature). We think that this is a poor way of writing theology on the subject of Mary, and we cannot see how one who uses this method can avoid the principle which appears on every page of Scripture, namely the freedom of purpose in the grace of God, and the free and *positive* character of all that follows from having chosen Him. There are others whose present activities in biblical research and traditional theology make it probable that their numbers will grow, whose Marian theology is the fruit of the elaboration of facts of *analogies of faith* which they apply to the mystery of

---

write on modern devotion. For any suggestion on this subject cf. *Irénikon,* XXIII (1950), pp. 178-182.

the "economy" or to the purpose of the grace of God, which is
the essential object of the testimony of Scripture as interpreted
in Church tradition.[51] Another theologian makes this specification:
"One can add almost anything to the mystery of the Virgin's
maternity, but one can hardly *take anything away.*" [52]

We think that all the excesses we are going to point out can
be referred to this incorrect way of theologizing. We can add that,
at least according to our own estimates, the definition of the
Assumption, because of the absence of explicit biblical texts from
which it would be possible to "deduce," oblige the theologian
to proceed in a roundabout way, and plunge into a more profound
Scripture research based on the *connections* between the great
biblical *themes;* it is impossible to "think" theologically about
the dogma of the Assumption without discovering that it lies at
the *point of contact between ecclesiology, christology, and eschatology.* The best works on this dogma, published about the time
of its definition, are orientated in this direction. The "new"
dogma, far from favoring a Mariology enclosed "in a vase," will
reintegrate mariological research into the entity of tradition. The
speculative era, that opened with the definition of 1854, and was
above all deductive, ended with the 1950 definition which turned
the movement into a reintegration of Marian truths, including
the *Immaculate Conception,* the truth which is explicitly contained in traditional facts, *divine maternity itself being put back
into its integral biblical and patristic context.*[53]

Once the above thoughts are clear, it will be easy to understand that it is here not a question of denying any specific point
discovered in Mariology, but of inserting it into an entity whose

---

51. Y. Congar, *Dieu vivant,* No. 18, (1951), pp. 109-110.
52. R. Laurentin, *Le mouvement Mariologique a travers le monde,* in
Vie Spirituelle, Feb. 1952, p. 183.
53. *Irénikon,* XXV, (1952), p. 369 and cont. to be taken in the context
of the whole article.

significance depends above all on the dynamic process of the perspective where one stands, and the centrifugal movement which animates the partial truths. It will suffice to enumerate some of the dangers which threaten Mariology (as all theology for that matter).

Beware of *isolating* certain aspects. It has often happened that out of a deep and original spiritual experience entire Marian treatises have grown; in such a case theology is too subservient to piety, whereas it should on the contrary be inspired by theology. This is not a positive, but a negative error through the omission of connected truths which should equilibrate each other and color any truth experienced by a spiritual witness.

The tendency that has been called "spiritual theology" (this term again may lend itself to ambiguity)[54] becomes more marked in some pious reviews in which only one aspect of Mary being considered, e.g. her mediation, use a vocabulary *without explanations which* the greater part of the readers cannot grasp, and which therefore lends itself to equivocation. Here are some literal quotations: "Every time when at the revival of the sacrifice on Golgotha the name Jesus is spoken I connect it in thought with that other name God has willed inseparable from it... *through Jesus Christ our Lord, through our Lady, Mary, His Mother.*" Everyone is at liberty to associate in his mind the name of Mary with that of Jesus when Mass is celebrated; nor do we state that such words imply a heresy, but we cannot but be impressed that as they now stand, the italicized words form an epigraph, and when printed symmetrically on two lines exactly above each other, create an equivocation in the mind of the reader; it is dangerous to seem to be putting side by side, or to join the *sacerdotal* mediation of Jesus, turned from humanity towards the Father, and Mary's prayer, *ad Christum* and not *ad Patrem,* as it

---

54. Y. Congar, *Tradition and Traditions in the Church* and *Rev. Sc. phil. theol.* 1951, No. 4, p. 624.

might appear from the symmetry of the two sentences. Should one not exercise more prudence in disseminating calendars in which for every month there is a picture representing Marian feasts grouped around a central picture, also of Mary? It is a pity that there is no reproduction referring to the feast of Easter, or if there is it is a *Pietà* which in itself does not fix attention on the glorious *resurrection*. Is there not danger in this of decentralizing the piety of those who use these calendars? Catholics, it will be said, will replace the hierarchic emblems in their right order: this may be so, but we are doubtful; and would it not be preferable to avoid surprising, and even shocking our separated brethren by such wide-spread excesses? And finally, is it not to be desired that the *sobriety and piety* the Vatican Council speaks of with reference to theology should be practiced everywhere, and that a correct hierarchy of Christian truths, including Marian truths, be immediately apparent, even in propaganda leaflets and calendars?

Another deviation by excess consists in arranging Marian truths into a too rigid system, hermetically closed in itself.

One of the best informed theologians [55] has recently brought up the question with reference to problems such as "the beatific vision conferred on Mary at the first moment of her conception," and of the use of her reason at the first moment of her life. Has not the tradition which considers this "beatific vision" probable, followed too servilely a systematical method of deduction? Would it not be better, since the Gospel texts show a true spiritual progress in Mary, to keep to the "hypothesis that the richness of the grace in Mary did at least hasten to awaken her reason (as the intellectual development of some saints was advanced in their childhood) and that from that moment on a mystical impetus carried the soul of Mary towards God; — it was perhaps

---

55. R. Laurentin, *Histoire de la théologie Mariale,* in *Vie Spirituelle,* Nov. 1952, pp. 398-399.

veiled and unconscious, — but profound and whole?" As a pure hypothesis the doctrine of the Immaculate Conception cannot mean that Mary, unlike the saints, had not known a spiritual progress? The doctrine which says that Mary was conscious of a mystical life from the first moment of her conception should be made consistent with that other which sees "three radically different grades of grace in her existence." [56]

In our opinion if all Mariology, and *a fortiori*, all theology is focused on the adage, *ad Jesum per Mariam*, the other adage should be used as abundantly and equally correlatively, for it is just as true (and in our opinion even more true) to say *Ad Mariam per Jesum*. If the theologian uses these two lines of approach symmetrically, the lack of balance we have already mentioned between the central position given to the intercession of Mary, and the no less central and *unique* position given to the mediation of Jesus, can be avoided: *Unus mediator, homo Christus Jesus.*

The third danger by excess lies in an *undue exaggeration* of certain aspects of Marian *piety*. While one should beware of minimizing the *parentic* importance of apparitions and miracles of the Virgin; one should at the same time beware of confusing these with the authentic sources of Marian doctrine in *ecclesial* tradition, or in the Bible.

The apparitions and the "revelations" of the Virgin (as a matter of fact those of Christ or any of the saints) belong into a "private" order; they can contribute to the spiritual wealth of the faithful of the Church, and can even (and do at times) help in a way to achieve a certain progress in understanding theological truths that have been discovered elsewhere in tradition, but they in themselves *are not theological* sources. Need we remind the reader that the words of the Virgin were spoken to Bernadette at Lourdes not before, but *after* the 1954 definition. *Theological*

---

56. Bouyer, *art. cit.*, pp. 153-155.

judgment of these phenomena would only gain by what St. Paul said of the *Charismata* of Corinth: *Aemulamini charismata meliora.* Here again, instead of maximizing it changes the point of focus.[57]

The three dangers we have indicated, to isolate, to systematize and to maximalize, often carry with them a fourth, the gravest, namely to court error, if not positively, at least in those imponderabilities which make the climate of a spiritual life. The most frequent error here can be twofold: the first is to suppose that Jesus is still too far from us, and that therefore we need a mediator between him and us; the second is to see in the Savior too exclusively the "God, the just and terrible Judge."

When all is said and done the danger here is a certain practical form of "Monophysitism," very subtle, but none the less extremely dangerous, for it is impossible to build a coherent *and true* Mariology on a Christology which leaves in the shadow, and even seems to forget "the most incontestable statement of the New Testamental revelations on the subject of Christ" (*Hebr.* 2, 10-11, 16-18; 4, 14-16), namely on the subject of the perfect "humanity" of Christ who has come to save that which had been lost, as "High Priest chosen amongst men and capable to feel compassion for their infirmities."

Father Congar, from whom these lines are borrowed, enumerates in *Tradition and Traditions in the Church,* examples of this deviation in texts (perhaps partly apochryphal) by St. Bernard, Olier, Nouet, and even in the impressive book of J. Guitton. He points out that in certain forms of scientific Mariology, which may

----

57. In *Nouv. Rev. theol.* LXXXIV (1952), Fr. Dhanis replies to the "Maximalist" critics of some theologians on his book regarding Fatima. The attitude Fr. Dhanis takes seems to us a model to be followed because of its same balance between the respect due to extraordinary phenomena, and a sense for theological methods; the attitude of his opponent seems to us typical of the temptation to maximalize of which we are speaking.

be very interesting, there is the same latent danger.[58] We agree with him that this road is absolutely barred, and we even see an indication here of what we have said regarding the connections between Mariology and Christology, it is because some theologians from the 17th century on use this Mariology marked by a certain exclusivism (e.g. Bérulle and Condren, who can only see one aspect of the Incarnation, the inner annihilation being carried so far that one seems to forget the psychological life of the *human nature* of Jesus) that their Mariology is not always well-balanced. The *Treatise on true devotion to the Holy Virgin,* though it seems at times, especially in its wording, to verge on a certain exclusivism, nevertheless contains such phrases as; "In order to come to Jesus we must go to Mary, she is our mediator by *intercession;* to come to *our Father* we must go to Jesus, for he is our *mediator by redemption.*[59] This text, in its "general principles" is full of true theological sense that one feels cannot always be found in all the present day Mariologists.

---

58. A critical and technical exposé in *Rev. Sc. phil. theol.* 1951, No. 4, pp. 626-629. The same exposition, but more easily available to the general public is in *Le Christ, Marie et l'Église,* pp. 80-88. L. Bouyer, *art. cit.* pp. 139-144 says the same, namely that Mariology is a test of Christology, for a healthy ecclesiology (for us Mariology is implied therein). Cf. in R. Aubert, *Problèmes de l'unité chrétienne,* Jan. 1953, p. 99 where this importance of Christology is emphasized. The book by J. Guitton, impressive and important as it is, sometimes gives the impression of a leaning towards a certain Monophysitism, e.g. p. 164; "Between Christ and us there exists an *infinitely great distance,* and we are inclined to seek how this could be diminished. It is here that the thought of Mary appears." No single line should ever be written about the Virgin without having first considered the essential elements in Christology.

59. *Traité de la vraie dévotion,* paragraph 86. Other passages, which at first might offer difficulty, should be interpreted by this paragraph. They are: 85, 130, 217, 221, 224, 225, 270, 273. In order to grasp the true meaning of this book its vocabulary should be disregarded for it bears the marks of its time and is not always traditional, (though still better than

The passage in Péguy, where the poet explains to his friend Lhote that he could no longer say, "Thy will be done" in the Our Father, but that in spite of all he could still manage to say the "Hail Mary," should not be wrongly interpreted; it does not mean that when one can no longer pray to God, one can still pray to Mary, this would be equivocal, since the prayer to Mary is in the end addressed to the Father, but simply that psychologically it is sometimes easier for one "who does not want to pray for a piece of bread" to pray through Mary in the angelic salutation.[60]

---

what we find on this subject in many a modern booklet); it should also be remembered that it was written as a reaction against the Jansenite minimization of Marian devotion of the time. The danger is at present rather the contrary, that is to say of a maximalization without any regard to the theological entity. It would be an exaggeration to take the book by St. Grignon de Montfort as a pattern to follow on every point. We also point out that, much as the general principles seem sound in this *traité*, in their applications they seem to show a leniency towards a too exclusively "privileged spiritual experience" which is certainly genuine, but too much of a reaction against Jansenism (in which at this point not everything was wrong), and with a view to an immediate and popular piety. The spiritual movement in the Legion of Mary, in spite of its militant and rather Irish vocabulary, seems to us *one* of the means for revitalizing the supernatural apostolate in Christians; moreover the value in the spirituality of the Legion lies in that it is open in Mary on two sides — towards the Holy Spirit and towards the Church. The spirituality of the Legion could be written in a more "technical" style, for example by pointing out that every time it is said that everything should be done "in Mary," this does not so much mean the individual historical person, as the part she plays in the providential economy of the perfect figure and image of the Church. To say "in Mary" also means (though not exclusively) "in the Church, through her." Read L. Suenens', *Theologie de l'Apostolat de la Légion de Marie*, 3rd ed. Bruges, 1953, and also *Une héroine de l'Apostolat, Edel-Mary Quinn*, Bruges, 1952, where a concrete testimony of Marian apostolate can be found in the line of the Legion.

60. It will suffice to point to the dangers of sentimentality in all the subjects of Mariology. What are we to think of an article on the Mass

CONCLUSION

Of the above two dangers which threaten theology and Marian piety, the too little and the too much, the latter is at present the greater. We should simply like to point out the essential in this too brief survey.

Mariology has arrived at a turning point. The time has come to orientate Marian piety as well as theology towards a reintegration, not by making it poorer, but by giving it more ample treasures within the entity of revealed mysteries, as suggested by *living* tradition. To minimize the role of the Mother of God in the economy of salvation would simply amount to eliminating one of its pillars; Christology and ecclesiology would suffer. But conversely, not to integrate Mariology into "economic" theology, but to develop it like a hothouse plant would be an *impoverishment of Mariology itself,* and gravely injure both Christology and ecclesiology, and from both these disciplines towards Mariology.

From the survey we gave of the non-believing world it became apparent how immense is the role of Mary in the psychological

---

headlined: "Come on, Mummy, the bells ring for Mass!" What can one say of a report recently submitted in which Christmas "is the feast of Mummy"? Cf. *Rev. Nouvelle*, Dec. 1952, pp. 481-487, where the liturgical, therefore traditional significance of "Christmas-Epiphany, unique mystery of the Incarnation" is explained. Finally mistrust "approximates," which are very ambiguous in some authors writing on the Assumption. Mauriac writes that the definition of 1950 was a "revelation." Graham Greene declares in *Life* that "while the resurrection of Christ can be regarded as the resurrection *of a God*(!) the resurrection of Mary predicts the resurrection of every one of us." (Quoted by Y. Congar in *Tradition and Traditions in the Church*). Except for some pages in *Journel d'un curé de campagne,* by Bernanos, and the admirable *Eve* by Péguy there is little in literature on Mary, at least little that is of any value. As for the English-speaking countries, the collection *Marian Studies,* Washington (of this ten volumes have appeared between 1950 and 1959), provides material for work.

and historical fields. It is all the more important that the reply given to the modern aspirations for "the ideal woman," her gentleness and love, be not inspired by sentimental or systematical considerations, which are at times questionable, but by the integral source of all theology, that is to say by revealed truth. One should beware of thinking that Mariology is an easy subject, either for preaching or for study, and that one can more or less say anything as long as it sounds "pious." Mariology, which is about to be developed fully, is a *difficult* field in theology, for it lies at the point where in theology several essential lines of thought cross. In other words it is impossible to study Mariology without at the same time studying (and sometimes more profoundly) Christology, ecclesiology and eschatology.

The survey we gave of the opinions of our separated brethren on Mariology will have, we hope, shown that theology must be aware of their positions, especially that of Orthodoxy, in order to achieve a well-balanced integration of Mariology into Christology, and that of the Reformed Churches for a more marked precision and theological doctrine. The time of easy polemics, often unjust and unprecise, is over.

Doubtless catechists and professors who read these pages will estimate that they are difficult. We would not deny this. Much as we desire that Mary, the Mother of God, the New Eve, and the eschatological image of the Church should be made known by preaching and teaching, we desire, since it is the desire of the Mother of the Savior herself, that this preaching take us to Christ. Did not Mary herself say to the servant at the wedding at Cana: "Do as he tells you"? [61]

----

61. It is important not to identify the statements made by isolated Protestant theologians with the central trend of the Reformed Churches. Their main line of thought will always be their concern to remind you of the biblical theme of "the unique mediator, the man Jesus Christ" and the unique "redeemer." Most Protestant theologians — with whom the Anglicans

agree — would say jokingly that the best way to say that there is but one mediator, one Redeemer is by not starting off with an ambiguous vocabulary in which Mary is called mediator and co-redeemer, for this amounts to saying that there are in fact two redeemers. No Catholic Mariologist would think or say this. But the Protestant will argue that the words "mediator," "co-redeemer" are so ambiguous in themselves that if applied to Mary they are bound to cause fatal misapprehensions in the minds of Christians.

So much to describe the Protestant's state of mind and his legitimate fears; it remains that the reintegration of Protestant thought into Marian themes proceeds along absolutely different lines than those of mediation and co-redemption; it rather turns toward a *rapprochement* between Mary and the Church under the sign of her who is the model of the acceptance of salvation. One can ask whether in face of this explicit reserve *which subsists even if the psychology of controversy can be overcome,* should not the discretion of a St. Leo, who at the Council of Chalcedon wished for no definition of faith, be regarded as an inspiration for Catholic Mariologists? Would it not be theologically, and also ecumenically, wiser to leave such aspects as "mediation, co-redemption, and the royalty of the Virgin" at the stage of the *theologoumena* which are legitimate theological opinions within a living Christian tradition, but unless there are grave and urgent dangers (though it is difficult to see such) it is more traditional not to turn them into defined dogmas (Note from 1962).

CHAPTER II

DOCTRINAL ORIENTATIONS
AND CATECHISTIC PERSPECTIVES

MARIOLOGY is a principle of light and a factor of balance for the rest of Christian doctrines. At its origins the reality of Mary's maternity was levelled against the docetic teaching which tried to deny Christ's human nature; later the title *Theotokos* (Mother of God) was an occasion for defining the divinity of Christ; this state of affairs continued until the recent definition of the Assumption drawn up explicitly to affirm faith in the divine destiny of man and in the resurrection of his body by designating Mary as the model for redeemed humanity as it marches towards its triumphal end. In a word, just as the Virgin is the "handmaid of the Lord," so Mariology is in a way the servant of theology, and those who, especially in the 19th century, put an end to this mission by placing it into a closed sphere, by doing so caused misery and sterility. Ever since the 17th century a deep gulf has divided theology from Mariology. Thanks to the *rapprochement* between Mary and the Church there now appears a possibility of a better balance in the tendency of a too excessive assimilation of Mary with Christ.[1]

---

1. We will quote our principal sources by initials. The four chronicles by R. Laurentin in *Vie Spirituelle*, Feb., March, May, Nov., 1952 — L, I,

The fact that the gulf we mentioned above, which divided Mariology from theology, is gradually bridged seems the most important point to be mentioned in this essay on doctrinal orientation; nevertheless it must be remembered that Mariology is in the full swing of its development, and that the subject is a difficult one. We will limit ourselves to point out such aspects as appear sufficiently stable to serve professors of religion and catechists for fixed points of departure. There will therefore be no personal synthesis, *a fortiori* new ideas are not to be expected; finally no arguing on the most audacious hypotheses which have so far been put forward, for example on the co-redeemer merits *de condigno*.[2] We will on the contrary try to outline some fundamental information on Mariology.

I. METHODOLOGY AND GENERAL ORIENTATIONS

Regarding *methodology* we have two observations. The first is to call to mind the two approaches to the Marian mystery — the Old and the New Testaments and ecclesiastical tradition.

The teacher should have current knowledge of the general meaning of texts, and specifically of the Old Testament *themes* which are the foundation of Marian revelation in the New Testament.

II, III, IV; Y. Congar, *Bull. theol.* . . . , in *Rev. Sc. phil.* theol. 1951 No. 4. — C. II; Y. Congar, *Réflexions sur l'Assumption in Dieu vivant*, No. 18, 1951 — C, III; L. Bouyer, *Le culte de la Mère de Dieu dans l'Église Catholique*, in *Irénikon*, XXII (1949) 2 B; J. Guitton, *La Vierge Marie* — G; our article on *Tradition and ecumenism*, in *Irénikon*, XXV (1952) — TO. Our initial quotation comes from L, IV, pp. 400-401 and L, II, pp. 295 and 303.

2. L. I. pp. 180-184 shows clearly the strong and the weak points of this theory. Since the bibliography listed on p. 249, No. 1 refers in the majority to very complete Marian chronicles beside some exceptions, we will refrain from quoting the complete references of authors, for they can be found in L and C I.

Mary stands at the key point between the old and the new economy; on the one hand she is the supreme flower of the *human* preparation (though realized in grace)[3] of the cradle destined to receive the Messiah; on the other she represents, after Jesus, "the consent and the cooperation of the Church." [4]

Moreover the texts of the New Testament, especially of Matthew and Luke, should be understood and proposed in their literal sense; it is important that the student be made to realize (in the Newmanian sense) that historical personality of the Virgin who must be shown rooted in Adamic humanity.[5] Thus a one-sided presentation of the Virgin, in which she figures exclusively in the mystery of liturgy and in patristic tradition, can be avoided. While speaking of the magnificent figure "the woman with a crown of twelve stars about her head," as she stands in the *Apocalypse*, the modest self-effacing young girl of Nazareth, filled with attentive fervor, as she is seen by the Synoptics, should also be evoked. Provided this is correctly interpreted we advise not to show only the eminent privileges of the Virgin, for example her divine maternity, and the same time neglect her historical humanity, for by doing so the same error would be committed as by emphasizing exclusively Christ's divinity. But here the error would be worse, since Mary was and has remained a creature. We think it is necessary to point out that there was progress in the holiness of Mary, as in her comprehension of divine mysteries which took place in her; the texts of the Synoptic Gospels are explicit on this subject.[6]

Besides this the professor should also teach Mariology using the second road of approach, i.e. *theological tradition* in liturgy

---

3. B, p. 155.

4. C, III. pp. 111-112.

5. G, pp. 25-82 gives a good exposition of this viewpoint. It should be combined with pp. 137-189 where A. writes on the mystery of Mary.

6. B, p. 154 and G, pp. 25-82.

and in the Fathers. He must show that although Mary appears immutable in eternity, her presence is not a going away, but an enveloping, somewhat in the way a circle would encompass our terrestrial and temporal world. Transcendence does not mean a withdrawal to a remote distance but an envelopment: within the most perfect envelopment, that of Christ, are other spheres, among them that of the Virgin.[7]

Doubtless the difficulty here lies in the changing over from the historical human creature to that celestial being who is represented in piety and dogma. This difficulty is already met with in the study of Jesus Christ; in Mariology both pictures must be accepted as equally true. We should remember that for the Christian eternity has already begun, though it may not yet be fixed, and that the mystery of eternity is that of a person who is at last formed, we can realize that the idea of our being is already achieved in secret, at least in substance, through grace. In Mary, Immaculate and fully redeemed, this "eternal idea" and "personality" was hidden during her terrestrial life. Her passage to everlasting life is but a manifestation of what she *had already* been here on earth.

Students should be made to understand clearly that this double image of the Virgin, the one within time and the other in eternity, are but one in the eyes of God, and that the life of Mary is but the change from this hidden envelopment of the image to its glorious manifestation; by this they can understand the essential law in the economy of supernatural faith, which is that eternity has already begun within time.[8]

One can now understand the importance of using the two sources of theology which, side by side, teach us the truth about Mary. The one relates to the "historical" life of the Mother of God,

---

7. G, pp. 209-211 and 237 ff.
8. G, pp. 137-146.

and the other to her "transhistorical," supernatural, and hidden significance — "the mystery of Mary."

The second remark on methodology tries to specify the significance of tradition in Mariology. While the first group of Marian truths, those on Mary within history, are chiefly based on the Synoptic Gospels, the second is rooted in the Johannine tradition of which we shall speak later.

It is to be hoped that the 1950 definition, if correctly interpreted, will help to build up a well-balanced Mariology. The "new dogma" obliges us to examine more thoroughly the *connections between* the mysteries and their harmony with the ultimate end of man, such as they appear in Scripture and tradition; for this, after all, is the normal function of theology. But since, just as in the case of the Assumption, the method of immediate and explicit literality being impossible because neither the Scripture nor the tradition of the first seven centuries gives explicit information about this truth, the theologian is obliged to seek his criteria in the *analogy of faith*.[9] This means that an exposition on Christ, the Holy Spirit and the Church must be made in such a manner that the role of Mary be apparent, and vice versa. A Marian exposition must be such that in it christological, ecclesiological, and pneumatological implications be immediately clear. This amounts to saying that Marian theology must govern Marian spirituality, and not the other way around.[10]

Our ideas will doubtless become clearer when we say that the 1950 definition should give us a better understanding of the other mysteries in the economy of salvation. The Assumption of Mary appeared to the Church closely bound to the other Marian truths, the divine maternity and the Immaculate Conception, but beyond these to other truths in faith, so that to deny the Assumption would endanger these essential verities. The *criterion* of good

---

9. C, III, p. 110.
10. C, I, p. 624.

mariological teaching can be expressed in the following; though there are differences, no definite separation should be made; it is necessary to "distinguish in order to unite"; Mariology is the pivotal point, "the microcosmos which reflects the macrocosmos of the general theology of the Incarnation, grace and the Church." [11] A good teacher must speak of Mary in such a manner that the student can understand the connection between the truths of salvation. The two great lines of thought we must follow before we can outline the synthesis are both open to the "macrocosmos" of theology.

The essential doctrinal orientation therefore follows from this general methodology. In one sense, because it is open to theological disciplines, no specialized Marian teaching is necessary for preaching or catechetics; the main theme of a sermon should lead straight to what is essential in the mysteries, and show their *supernatural connections,* in each case landing us at the general economy of salvation and at its Marian aspects.

II. THE FIRST CREST-LINE: "MATER DEI"

The Annunciation realizes the Incarnation of the divine Word in a human nature. The sources thereof are on the one hand the Synoptic texts, on the other the definition made in 431. [12]

In the Annunciation there are two elements, one is the divine choice of Mary, the call of the angel, the other the answer *fiat,* which represents human cooperation in the incarnation of the divine principle of our salvation.

The theme of this *call* is there throughout the entire Old Testament; it includes the choice of individual persons, Abraham and Moses, and that of an entire people, Israel, "the People of God."

11. G, p. 133.
12. C, I, p. 624.

It can however be noted that the call to an individual is always made within a call *to an entity* in the Bible; Abraham, Moses or the prophets were chosen from and for the salvation of the People of God. Mary was chosen by God, but even her choice can be placed within a general framework of choosing God's people, at least chronologically, for ontologically this choice was made earlier; it is the *archetype* of the call to the people of God, the image of the Church. The Annunciation is therefore the *crowning* of earlier "annunciations"; it is the transposition onto a higher plane, differing from the earlier choices not only in degree, but also in nature. It is, we might say, transfiguration, for here it is a case of a choice *for divine maternity*. Whereas the prophets were testimonies of the divine Word throughout oral or "sacramental" manifestations, Mary is the tabernacle of the *substantial*, personal, and divine Incarnation of the Word come down to dwell among us. The hypostatic union in Jesus Christ is the basis of the call to the Mother of God, the mother in the flesh. It is around this divine maternity, in the very heart of the work of salvation, that the mystery of Mary has developed, since the resurrection, the Church, the gift of the Spirit, and the eschatological glory are all extensions of the Incarnation.[13]

Students should be made to see this clear line of thought which began with the mysterious presence of God in the shining cloud in the desert, and led to the passage in John: "The Word pitched His tent and came to dwell among us";[14] but at the same time it should be shown how in Mary, the Mother of God, there took place a change to an absolutely transcendental plan, that is to the full meaning of the essential divine initiative of the Incar-

---

13. The turning point here came in the twelfth century. It is from this epoch that the text of the "pseudo-Augustin," which had so great an influence, seems to date. Cf. L. IV, p. 393.

14. Remember the term *eskènôsen* used by John; it alludes to the tent of the Tabernacle onto which the shining cloud descended.

nation whose earlier movements were but forecast shadows in its preparation.

In the mystery of the Annunciation, too, there is a response, a *fiat*. Mary's answer is not merely psychological, we could say that it was also ontological because it affected the full being, God's creature who in grace, and by its acceptance, became once again *creator* in its original integrity; for though Mary is Mother, she remains a *virgin* in her very maternity.

It is important here to recall an essential point in faith: Humanity is a likeness of God in that it is not a dead object but a living subject which, however paradoxical this may sound, is called on to take part in its own creation, in as much as it is its task to accomplish its own perfection. For example, the fecundity of humanity is the very characteristic which contains the divine image, since it is what makes it *creative and at the same time remains a creature*. Creation, issued from God, is so very deeply "creation" that it gives man the gift of being "creator," although in a similar and dependent, nevertheless real sense; which allows him to say, "God has need of man." But ever since the first sin "human fecundity is fundamentally *ambiguous*, for generation propagates, inextricably and confusedly, both life and sin, that is to say death." While this fecundity continues to affirm our divine origin, it also carries us back to the mere animal level. This is bound to the fact, so clearly stated by St. Paul, that while the bodily state of man is holy and a glorification of God, the flesh is sinful and is an instrument of the devil. To put this more clearly: life cannot any longer propagate itself in the Adamic humanity without the same time suffering a disruption — the being who transmits life cannot do this without wounding his own integrity, and the being achieved thereby is by its birth a separate being. As Origen says, *"ubi peccatum, ibi multitudo."*

Mary, being a *Virgin* Mother, represents here the *original integrity;* in her the creature returns to being a "creator" without any ambiguity, and *without tearing the original integrity.* So she *is,* not only in her thought and her love, but in her *being* a Virgin Mother, the perfect answer of the creature, the human cooperation willed by God in the great work of life and sanctification; she realizes her divine maternity as a creature from her place at the summit of humanity's vocation. Her special grace is not only that she is virgin, and the purest of all virgins, but that she is virgin in her very maternity. Her maternity implies no blemish nor does it diminish her; far from giving birth to another element in a fully dissociated humanity, she brings to light the New Adam in whom and through whom "all the dispersed children of God shall be united into one single body." The full glory of the Virgin "is all concentrated in the fact that she is Mother of the Savior, that is, she is at the same time a return to the original integrity of creation as it issued from the hands of the Creator, and the achievements of the supreme end He projected for her. By the perfect *answer* of her created initiative to the creating initiative, mankind becomes once again as God conceived it, and this deed brings into the world the perfect product of the *common* work of man and God, the God-Man." [15]

Both aspects, that of the Annunciation and of the Incarnation are reflected on the liturgical text: *Rorate coeli desuper et nubes pluant iustum; aperiatur terra et germinet Salvatorem.* This sentence sums up all the Old Testament in Mary. It also shows that humanity really cooperates in the work of salvation, that is to say when God gives, He gives really *something;* the creature becomes "himself" in his receptivity, he becomes the reception; but this receptivity is *creative.*

It is the motion of creation itself that should here be further investigated by the catechist; God gives to the creature "the quality of being a substance, to be active and to fulfill his end."

---

15. B, pp. 143-144. The professor should base his arguments here, as B, does, on texts of the antiphons of Circumcision, the feast of Christmas celebrated in a Marian atmosphere.

The condition of the creature is not passivity, but active receptivity; ontological participation is in the active and "creative" power of God himself; the doctrine of the divine image calls essentially for this aspect. This creative receptivity is also verified on the plane of grace. One should therefore also stress the idea that the *fiat* Mary spoke was entirely a gift of God, and this safeguards the transcendence of divine initiative. It is a real gift, that is to say God's action penetrates the natural and supernatural being so deeply, that it will be given him to cooperate in the work of creation and redemption. There is therefore no question of a Pelagian cooperation between man and God here, but simply a vision of the ontological and supernatural depth and breadth of the work of Jesus.

We have arrived at one of the cardinal points in theology. We mentioned at the beginning; what is involved in the mystery of the Annunciation under the aspect of the *fiat* is the role humanity has to play in the work of redemption. Over the horizon of these essential thoughts on Mary's divine maternity looms the "Monophysitist" danger we have already discussed in Christology (wherein the acts of will and knowledge of the human in Jesus are minimized), in ecclesiology (wherein only supernatural structures would be welcome) and in Mariology (wherein only the choice of supernatural privileges would be stressed, and human cooperation in the *grace of the Mother* of God, neglected).[16]

While there is in the divine maternity a divine choice and a human response (in grace), and while this response is the perfect accomplishment of the vocation of a creation called on to act a part of a "creator," on earth as in sanctification, there is also a central truth in Mariology which now looms above the horizon: "free intercourse with divine grace, by virtue of which we have

16. C, II, the whole, but above all the first chapter, is conceived in this sense.

the duty to work out our own salvation (although it is always God who works in us the willing and the acting), *will never exist in us otherwise than enveloped in, and as it were engaged by the will whose perfect realization remains the Virgin Mother.* Mary's holy and believing freedom will perpetually engender ours. There is no human faith which can accept grace otherwise than if man models his faith on hers, and allows himself to be carried and absorbed by her faith.[17] Through her *fiat*, Mary *is the transcendent archetype of all the fiats* spoken by man in answer to the call of Christ, for both ways to redemption are perfectly realized therein; the gift of God and the free reply, the two uniting in the activity of supernatural creation by which God gives *Himself* totally to us and gives us the chance to accept Him freely in grace. Here is the espousal of God with man, the answer of humanity is enveloped, carried and *created* in a real freedom by the divine initiative itself.

In our opinion, one should beware of a dangerous extrapolation, such as is for example represented in the thesis of H. M. Köster (not to be confounded with M. D. Koster). This theologian, who has chosen Alexandrian Christology to which the sacerdotal mediator is the *divine Logos*, thinks that, since Jesus Christ has no human personality, he cannot fulfill the function of expressing the solidarity, the cooperation and the acceptance of the gift of God; there must therefore be "an open space" into which Marian mediation can be inserted, without thereby diminishing Christ's mediation. In this work of constituting the treasures of redemption Mary represents the part of the human *person*, the *active acceptance*. As both Laurentin and Congar have observed, there is here a danger of Monophysitism. At any rate what we have said above in no way implicates this theory by Köster.[18]

---

17. I, B, p. 145.

18. C, pp. 627-629 and L, II, p. 302. The greatest difficulty in Köster's theory is that he stresses strongly the bilaterality, thereby giving an impres-

The role of archetype recognized in the Marian *fiat*, in the human acceptance of the gift of salvation in us (but not in objective constitution of this gift)[19] will direct us from the first crest line from which we set out, towards divine Maternity, and lead us, to a second, the maternity of grace, at least in the sense that Mary is the model of humanity for all creative receptivity of a supernatural life.[20]

One could well ask if by delving into the theological significance of this *fiat* one would not arrive at the second crest line by the indirect way of what we term "sponsality." In the text, *et incarnatus est de Spiritu Sancto ex Maria Virgine*, some theologians, beginning with St. Bernard, seem to have discovered a theme which they expressed in the words *Sponsa Spiritus Sancti*. We would not, as a matter of fact, have chosen these words, for one can hardly see how they can be conjoint with another appellation, for older and above all more closely bound with central themes in ecclesiology; *Maria Sponsa Verbi*. One can also legitimately ask whether the importance of the *fiat*, that is to say of the creative cooperation of Mary in the center of the maternal mystery, does not imply a relationship of betrothal. This relationship is evidently closely bound to a "widened and integral maternity."

At the top of this first crest line we have thus found two central truths, one in Mariology and the other in *general theology*; firstly the absolute primacy in the project of divine choice, God alone being able "to give God," and God alone able to give man a natural and supernatural liberty, for he created and re-created him (in grace); and secondly the maternal consent, the pattern

---

sion of a kind of "conjunction" between Mary and Christ on the same plane. Semmelroth avoids these difficulties although he too, was influenced by Köster.

19. Cf. infra. pp. 269-271.

20. B, pp. 145-146.

of all our consents, the perfect realization of man's natural and supernatural vocation, image of God, that is to say the creative creature; these last words evidently interpreted in the precise sense we have shown.

The point where these two central truths meet is in Christology; it is the divine Word which is incarnate, freely, but into a human nature with human will and energy; this human nature, because it is, and in so far as it is, assumed ontologically in the divine person, operates salvation and becomes the "sacrament" of divinity. There is in Jesus both a divine and a human life, *conjoint, but not confused, distinct but not divided*. With obvious differences, the same two truths are found in Mariology and ecclesiology. There is no danger therefore of taking away from Christ what is given to Mary, since divine maternity orientates essentially towards the God-Man.

III. THE SECOND CREST-LINE: "SPONSA VERBI"

Here the high points are the Immaculate Conception and the Assumption. From the scriptural aspect the climate is rather that of the Johannine revelation, although these two dogmas appear more directly bound to the living Magisterium of the Church than is the Annunciation. It is chiefly since the turning-point in the 12th century that tradition has clarified these aspects of Marian mystery. In the Immaculate Conception as in the Assumption we are facing two facts, both of which belong to the positive economy and are freely willed by God. First we will go deeper into the Mary-Spouse theme, after that we will disclose the manifestation of the two above mentioned dogmas.

1. THE MARY-SPOUSE THEME [21]

This theme has two aspects: firstly Mary is associated with the principle of salvation not only at the historical moment of the Incarnation, but throughout the entire economy. Secondly Mary is the fecund spouse; that is to say through her maternity of grace she is mother of all the redeemed.

a) *Biblical themes*. It is here a question of themes and not of isolated texts, for it is within the play of connections between revealed themes, that by analogies in faith the picture of Mary as *Sponsa Verbi*, appears where these themes intersect.

The theme of the espousals is present throughout the entire Old Testament; it has bearings on Israel, the People of God whom the Bible calls the bride of Yahweh; but it also includes the individual soul of every member of the People of God. It seems to us that one of the peaks of the Old Testament, the one where a number of other lines of revelation conjoin, is expressed therein.

The picture of the espousals reappears again in the New Testament in the theme of the Church-spouse, mentioned by St. Paul, and in the *Apocalypse*: Christ is delivered so that the Church may appear as a wife without spot or wrinkle before God's throne; the sacrament of marriage is great "in relation to Christ and the Church"; finally the woman crowned with stars, with the moon at her feet, giving birth in pain is, besides other meanings, a picture of the Church.

Let us add finally that for the Old Testament the text of the *"protoevangelium,"* though it does not itself contain a picture of the Church, nevertheless expresses the idea of the descent of the woman who took part in the victory over the devil. Although the theme of the Spouse is not specifically there, neither is it excluded.

We have now recalled the first series of *explicit* biblical themes,

---

21. The words in this title are inspired by speculative Mariology. But as it will be seen, we believe they are founded in positive theology.

from the *Genesis* to the *Apocalypse;* a second series now appears which examines the first more thoroughly and reveals the *Marian implications* therein. This second series of themes comes from the Johannine revelations which in our opinion represent a summit in the New Testament. The Marian texts in the Gospel of John (2, 1-11; 19, 25-27) are connected on the one hand with verse 13 of the prologue and with the Genesis 3, 15, and on the other hand with Apoc. 12, and suggest that Mary, Spouse of the Word, is associated with the redemption and is the spiritual Mother of the faithful.

It is a question of connections between the various parts of the Gospel on the one hand, and between the Gospel and the *Genesis* and *Apocalypse* on the other. For example in the words "my hour has not yet come," spoken at Cana, there is a link between the mystery of the Cana *wedding* and the hour of the Cross. The mystery at Cana is an anticipation of the mystery on the Calvary; this latter, by manifesting the glory of Jesus, is also the foundation of the Church which was born beside the New Adam "who fell asleep on the Cross," and was given a new life in the two sacraments of the Spirit, in Baptism and the Eucharist. Mary was present here. But Mary was also present at Cana where the water changed into wine is the symbol of the Eucharist. The Cana *wedding* is a messianic wedding, a banquet of the Kingdom, for in St. John it takes place immediately after the baptism of Jesus in the Jordan where John the Baptist accomplished his mission as Precursor of the Kingdom.

This first bond between Cana and the Calvary twines around the theme of the glory of Jesus in his death, but this theme also signifies the birth of the Church, the New Eve born of the New Adam; Mary, who is present in these two *central* events in John's Gospel, is therefore mysteriously bound to the death which brings salvation, and is the foundation of the Kingdom; but she is also there at the nuptial banquet which founds the Church, the New Eve.

Doubtless the Bodmer papyri II and XV establish the fact that the original reading of John 1, 13 is *nati sunt,* and not *natus est* (this reading was denied in Ptolemaist gnosis). There is therefore no allusion to virgin birth here. This remark invites prudence and warns of the danger of schematizing or of setting out from preconceived conclusions. On the other hand the events up to the Cana wedding, being arranged by St. John *into seven days,* the words of the introduction, "At the beginning . . ." which are as a matter of fact an obvious allusion to the first verse of *Genesis,* it becomes clear that the first part of this Gospel which the inspired author focused on the testimony of John the Baptist and Mary, is the manifestation of *the new supernatural creation,* the return in Jesus to Adamic integrity. In other words the first part of John's Gospel *is a new Genesis,* it is the account of the new creation in Jesus.

Here we have arrived to two different arrangements of events: one is the part from Cana to Calvary; the prologue, Baptism to Cana, with the account of the creation in Genesis, is the other. A third group should be here mentioned, the one which binds the Gospel to the *Apocalypse* in the image of the star-crowned woman. This threefold connection shows that Mary is the woman, enemy of the serpent, Mother of the Savior and his associate in Redemption; this is the reason why St. John represents her simultaneously in two places (19, 26 and Apoc. 12, 17) as the Mother of the faithful. Moreover at the moment of writing he was already placing her in her *final place,* in her *glorious* aspect comparable only to the triumphant Lamb of God and the Heavenly Jerusalem.

If we now consider that this Heavenly Jerusalem is presented by John in the *Apocalypse,* clothed *like a bride* to meet her husband, and that all themes describe the mystery of God's espousals with the world in the Kingdom around a messianic banquet (though it is true that the Evangelist does not give Mary the title of *New Eve*), checking on these points it becomes clear that Mary is intimately associated with the New Adam. This is a basis for the title of New Eve which tradition (at least partly) accords to Mary. Here is the root of the Scripture title, *Sponsa Verbi*.[22]

b) *Traditional themes.* The passage from Johannine revelation to liturgy is easy; whereas in the first crest line liturgical solemnity is above all focused on Christmas-Circumcision, in the second, the feasts immediately present are the dedication feast of the Church, the Assumption (the new office) and the Immaculate Conception, then towering above these three solemnities, the Epiphany.[23]

Here the center of gravity is the mystery of *the Church*, whereas in the first crest line it was the *Incarnation*. Mary is here, as Semmelroth says, *Urbild der Kirche*,[24] Mary is the Church. And if the Church is the New Eve, Mary, who is the archetype of the Church, is also the New Eve. If the Church is the spouse of the Word, Mary, in virtue of her special right, is here also *Sponsa Verbi*. If the Church is our Mother, then Mary is too by virtue of her unique right. New Eve, Spouse, Mother of the faithful; all three titles can refer equally to Mary and to the Church.

Here is a line of thought which has left its mark on the most authentic tradition. While theologians have brought into light this connection between Mary and the Church only recently, this theme, as read in ecclesiastical tradition *is as old as Scripture itself*. But difficulties begin the moment a closer positive and speculative examination of the subtle relations and differences which exist between Mary and the Church is undertaken.

A first specification is that Mary is the Church within the order of *ontological holiness*, but not strictly speaking within *sacerdotal holiness*, for sacerdotal charisma is immediately and essentially

---

22. All this is inspired by F. M. Braun, *Marie, Mère des fideles. Essai de thèologie johannique*, Paris, Tournai, 1952.

23. TO, pp. 357-362 and our article *Noel-Epiphanie, unique mystère d'Incarnation* in *Revue Nouvelle*, Dec. 1952.

24. C, I, p. 625 also H. Rahner recorded in the same place.

bound to the humanity of the mediating Word.[25] Secondly it is
well to remember that Mary is not, like Christ, "a social person"
but "a person with a social mission." [26] This does not prevent us
from considering the Virgin as an individual historical person;
she must be seen in relation to the whole Christ; just as the center
of the economy is not the "historical Christ," but the whole Christ,
so, too, in the center of Mariology there is not the historical person
of Mary, but her person fulfilling "a social mission." [27] Thirdly,
there is an important difference between the way the East and
the West approach the theme Mary-Church. The East goes from
the Church to Mary (this appears to be more in conformity with
St. John) whereas the West goes from Mary to the Church.[28] This
will bring us to a fourth specification by Fr. Congar. Tradition
on the Eve-Mary theme has not yet been completely and precisely examined, and as it appears from the research of the moment there is on the one hand "a certain relation between Eve
and Mary, on the other there is the Pauline relation between Adam
and Christ, but for the Fathers the Church is the New Eve, as
the *spouse of the New Adam.* To the Fathers Mary is rather the
new Paradise." [29]

These still unsolved problems warn us to be prudent in using
this relation between Mary and the Church. Personally we would
prefer to go, as do the Easterns, from the Church, and New Eve,
to Mary; however this should in no way modify the reality of
the bonds which exist between the two aspects of the economy
of salvation. On both sides there is "receptive and creative femi-

25. Ch. Journet, *La définition solenelle de l'Assomption de la Vierge,*
Saint-Moritz, Switzerland, 1951. (Article reprinted from *Nova et Vera*
in brochure.)

26. L, I, p. 182.

27. C, I, p. 626.

28. L, II, p. 296.

29. C, I, p. 625, No. 79 and H. de Lubac, *Méditations sur l'église* (Coll.
Theol. No. 27) Paris, 1953, p. 273 ff.

ninity," [30] and on both sides there is *"espousal relationship"* (the association with the life giver and husband, the Word) maternal fertility (giving birth to Christ in the soul)[31] and efficacy of the Holy Spirit (who is the soul of the Church and the agent for the Incarnation *ex Maria*).[32] The advantage of this perspective is that it is easily assimilated by the faithful since it relates to *central* truths in the economy of salvation in our Mother the Church, the same time emphasizing Mary's part in this work. Finally is it not once again evident that if we put ecclesiology into the center of gravity, Mariology need not be enclosed in itself since the mystery of the New Eve, spouse of the Word, has no sense either in Mary or the Church except as related to the divine husband, the incarnate Christ?

We will add that this way to present the second crest line has been applied to the most important and valuable works recently.[33] Moreover one has seen in our sociological survey how this perspective meets the view of the East, the Anglican and Reformed Churches, at least in this sense that it admits Mary as a figure of the Church, though affirming its will to maintain Mary *within* the Church while the same time she surpasses it in a way it is difficult to specify theologically, but which is evident since it is object of two dogmas, the Immaculate Conception and the Assumption. Such an approach to dissident Christianism shows that this Mariology lies along the line of the "undivided Church." [34]

---

30. L, II, p. 299.

31. B, p. 145. But we can only attain this birth from the Holy Spirit by becoming ourselves participants, mystically, but really from the birth of Jesus, since the new creation this birth must produce is He Himself.

32. Cf. L. Suenens, *Theology of the Apostolate.*

33. L, II, pp. 295-304; C, I, pp. 624-629; B, p. 149 ff.

34. C, I, p. 626.

2. IMMACULATE CONCEPTION AND ASSUMPTION

We think it better to show first of all the general themes in which these two dogmas occur, since our method is to point out the connections between the mysteries so as to avoid a deductive theology which is a frequent danger in Mariology. It would however be completely wrong to infer from this that there is only a difference of degree between Mary and the Church. The Immaculate Conception and the Assumption show precisely that although Mary is the Church, she is that in a *different order*, that of being associated by virtue of a privileged title to Christ, the Author of Salvation. In other words while Mary is the image of the Church, she is her image as a *transcendent archetype*.

Here we must go back to what we have said regarding the first crest line, to *divine and virginal* maternity, for in it are rooted the other two glories of Mary, the Immaculate, who was raised into heaven. Virginal maternity is in the order of unique privileges, and *as such is incommunicable;* by virtue of it she belongs to a related order (we do not say an order similar to, or identical with), that is to say that the hypostatic union which is as we have said above, also incommunicable. Doubtless Mary is "immaculate," *ex praevisis meritis Christi;* [35] and as we have said above this is a cardinal fact. But through the virginal integrity of her maternity, as through the fact that she is the Mother of God, the tabernacle where the New Adam was born, Mary by her *unique* grace sign belongs to the *order of the new creation;* she is in the order of that "new Paradise" which returns to, but also transcends, the first. We find here both the texts of Catholic liturgy wherein Mary is represented by the words "wisdom which presided at the constitution of the world, and was before ever

---

35. Historical proof of this part of the definition in L, IV, pp. 396-399 (where recent works on annexed questions are reviewed).

the world was," and the soul of Eastern liturgy wherein Mary
appears united with her Son within a special order.

a) *Immaculate Conception.* Now that the general aspects have
been outlined it will suffice to give the catechist ways of approach. The principle is that "from the beginning the Virgin
existed in an integrity belonging to God such as the Church can
only attain in the end. The Immaculate Conception does not
therefore dispense Mary from salvation, but she is *its first realization,* whose original perfection in Mary is for us the example
and pledge of what is to be the final perfection in us." [36]

Although neither our final perfection, nor that of the Church,
can ever equal *the personal* holiness of Mary, the Immaculate,
they are real participations, and in the ecclesial *economy* belong
to the same order. It is the same reality of bridal relationship
with God which is reflected by different rights by Mary, by the
Church, and by each individual soul. The dogma of the Immaculate Conception only stresses that in Mary this relation of belonging has a supereminent right, which is the basis of the cult called
"hyperdulia." It is well to point out to the faithful that the Immaculate Conception does not mean that the parents of the Virgin
conceived without concupiscence, and therefore had not transmitted to Mary the same life as any child of Adam, that is to say
"a life polluted at its source; this dogma signifies that from the
first moment of her conception the grace of Christ was working
in her, immediately redeeming her and lifting from her the male-
diction all sons of Adam have to hear." [37] Attention must be
drawn to the fact that the Immaculate Conception is not the same
thing as the "virginal conception" of Christ in Mary; this is still
a *very frequent* confusion. It is also useful to emphasize that
Mary's original integrity does not cancel the progress in her holy

---

36. B, p. 151.
37. B, pp. 152-153.

life.[38] Finally it is well to call attention to the fact that Mary's original holiness, *ex praevisis meritis Christi,* is no more of a problem than the sanctification of the righteous in the Old Testament (and we should like to add, of every soul of good will in other religions, both before and after Christ).[39] Since the beginning of time "the *Logos* dwelt among the children of man."

b) *Assumption. Mary is the eschatologic icon of the Church. At the origin of the Church, Mary presents, condensed in her own person, the perfection which must spread in the end among the multitude of believers assembled in the Unique.* She is thus the symbol and the pledge of Catholic unity.[40]

This dogma focuses all attention on the glorious Church at the end of all time, and on the salvation of the whole of man, body and soul. Whereas the dogma of the Immaculate Conception shows the Church rather as a reintegration of the first Adamic integrity, the Assumption has above all an *eschatological* bearing; eschatology being here interpreted in its full ecclesial abundance, co-extensive in time and space in the world, in soul and body, spirit and matter.

We would not advise professors to look for literal Scripture texts in order to deduce this dogma; they should also beware of making any illusion to the legendary end of the Virgin; in commenting on icons representing the Dormition, or pictures and sculptures of it; teachers should emphasize that these are symbols of a faith founded elsewhere on the living· tradition of the Church. The Bull *Munificentissimus,* is here the model. They should not stress any possible direct bond between the Immaculate Conception and the Assumption. We think it is better to show this dogma through a clear picture of the Church, which can transmit *realities,*

---

38. B, p. 154.
39. B, pp. 154-156.
40. B, pp. 150 and 156.

by tradition, and as a Bride, is assisted by the Spirit to interpret revealed deposits. Besides, we would also advise them to emphasize three things: firstly that Mary is the archetype of the triumphant Church; secondly that she is pre-eminently the one who defeated Satan (the applications to the modern world are here evident, to a point that the opportunity of the definition is justified in part by the Church's concern in strengthening her children's faith in the *victory* of God over the evil which appears almighty); thirdly, that through the assumption of her body the Virgin is already what we ourselves and the Church shall only be at the end of all time. Of these three aspects the eschatological seems to us the most important,[41] because Christians must be given back that *cosmic* sense of redemption, which has been completely lost in the West. Throughout the above insist on the fact that the Assumption shows in Mary the *integral* redemption *through the resurrected Christ*. In Mary the resurrection *of the Church is* anticipated, but it is founded on that of the Savior, Spouse of Mary and Spouse of the Church.

3. Mediation and Co-redemption

We are here leaving the sphere of truths defined by the extraordinary Magisterium in order to enter upon the life of the Church, as it is manifested in a series of beliefs whose exact theological bearings cannot as yet be gauged.

a) *Mediation.* Since Mary is the archetype of the Church, she possesses like it — and as well by virtue of her own supereminent title based on her *personal* privilege of Mother of God, — the power of intercession: this power cannot be exercised *apud Patrem,* but *apud Filium,* as we say in the prayer in the Mass of Mary the Mediator, which certain dioceses use. Saint Grignion

---

41. C, I, p. 620; *Construire,* VI (1951), pp. 58-61.

de Montfort could, it seems to us, be followed on this point when he writes that Mary is mediator through the *intercession* of her Son, while the Son is mediator of *Redemption* through the Father;[42] in other words Mary does not collaborate in the *constitution* of the wealth of salvation, which is the work of Jesus, the High Priest of the order of Melchisedech.

We ourselves would personally prefer the formula of de la Taille, the *omnipotentia supplex.* We suggest that the professor should emphasize the importance of the formula, *per intercessionem Mariae et omnium sanctorum,* which has the double advantage of showing the bonds of Marian intercession together with those of the triumphant Church, and of avoiding the word, difficult enough in itself, "mediator," which is not easy to reconcile with the *unus mediator homo Christus Jesus.* We even wonder whether the word "intercession" could not enable us to find a happier formula.

As for the "universal" character of Marian intercession, we suggest that it should be applied in the general context on the Church; in as much as she is "catholica," the Church offers *in Christo* a *universal* prayer for intercession; Mary, the archetype of the Church does the same, but *a fortiori in Christo.* But beware of giving the impression by these terms that Mary, as it were, intercedes directly with the Father; the only one who intercedes *apud Patrem* is Christ; the Church can reach the Father *through* Christ, for Christ is *the one who prays and offers.* We think that here Mary should above all be seen within the Church (of which besides she is the archetype). Finally avoid all vague expressions and specifications which might unduly anticipate the judgment of the Church; the professor should leave that to specialized theologians; it is desirable that preachers do the same.[43]

---

42. *Treatise on the true devotion,* Par. 86.
43. With respect to adages like "a child of Mary will not perish," these should be used with the greatest prudence, see L, II, p. 303.

b) *Co-redemption.* Together with Y. Congar, L. Bouyer and R. Laurentin, we confess we dislike this term and would prefer "associate" of Redemption; [44] as it stands this term might make us forget that "when God gives his grace to man (*gratia creata*) this gift is a means created by the gift by which he gives himself to man (*gratia increata*). Can a creature merit this with equivalence? [45]

This criticism seems to rule out fairly radically the recent theory on the merits of *de condigno congruo.* Would not these terms be better expressed by the words which are in our opinion preferable; "associate of the Redemptor, co-operator in redemption"? We think the answer is yes, *salvo iudicio meliori Ecclesiae.* Professors and preachers should refrain from using too new formulas.

However that may be regarding the term itself, which as a matter of fact the Church never permitted to penetrate into the liturgy (and this can be considered as an important indication, at least with respect to theological prudence) it seems that it should be allowed that Mary co-operates in Redemption subjectively, that is to say accepting salvation freely. As a matter of fact it is here the entire Mystical Body which is "co-redemptor."

Semmelroth specifies that the acceptance of redemption by the living entity of the Church was made at the time of the Passion by Mary, who is here a "receptive cause." There is therefore something more than a subjective co-redemption here, but it lies wholly in the order of the acceptance, leaving the part of the unique Redemptor clearly in the *constitution* of the wealth of grace. Since Semmelroth also avoids the "bilateralism" of the alliance suggested by Köster as well as his choice of a simple Alexandrian Christology, his hypothesis seems fairly fruitful.[46]

Bouyer insists on the fact that redemption cannot be accepted

---

44. C, I, p. 635, No. 79, L, I, p. 183 and B, p. 147.
45. L, I, p. 183 on the theory of merit as co-redemptrix *de condigno.*
46. C, I, p. 626 and L, II, p. 302.

passively, as if humanity was automatically undergoing it; there is no semi Pelaganism here, for the efficacy of *salvation* is precisely to redeem all the reality of creation; in the gift of God Himself the free action of man must have already been mysteriously included. Thereafter there is no redemption without suffering, and we can grasp the meaning of the Pauline words "we must work out our own salvation with fear and trembling, knowing that it is God who operates in us the will and the action." We can therefore understand "how the most holy Virgin, standing at the foot of the Cross, her heart pierced by the dagger of Simeon's prophecy, eminently represents this co-operation which the entire humanity must give for its own salvation, even if acquired through the sole virtue of its divine head."

"Marian co-redemption" is here in the same order as the redemption of the entire Mystical Body, according to the words of St. Paul on the sufferings of Christians who "complete" the sufferings of Jesus "in his body, that is to say the Church." Fr. Bouyer's thought, while rather stressing the "active and co-operative" in Mary (this is less evident in Semmelroth), shows very clearly the bond between the Marian and the ecclesial intercession which is itself bound to an integral conception of salvation giving man back "free and supernatural action." Bouyer joins Semmelroth here, and adds that the expression "co-redeemer" deserves to be applied to Mary in a special way, firstly because of the chronological and ontological order of her answer to grace, secondly because of her virginity and maternity (the result of the absence of sin in her), the generosity of Mary in "compassion" was absolutely "pure"; she has therefore a quality "absolutely *sui generis*," and for all that possessing a special virtue for the entity of the Mystical Body.[47]

Should one go further and speak of an "objective" co-redemp-

---

47. B, pp. 147-149.

tion? We will not enter into the question and will only quote
the opinion of a good theologian on the subject of Köster and
Semmelroth, who says that these authors give Mary *too much,*
in their tendency of making her role a sort of necessity, due to
some insufficiencies in Christ, and *too little* in that they restrict
Mary to a passive role which leaves her out of objective redemption. This theologian proposes the term "active communion." [48]
However that may be, it is better to keep away from this problem
in *ordinary* teaching and catechetics.

We can sum up the second point as follows: Mary is wholly
redeemed by Christ. The word "wholly" implies the Immaculate
Conception and the Assumption, this latter being seen more in
its eschatological incident; the word "redeemed" (in the sense
proper to Mary, *in instanti conceptionis, ex praevisis meritis
Christi*) shows the fullness of the redemption itself, while it
also implies the possibility in Mary of a real co-operation in the
work of salvation; finally the words "through Christ" affirm that
at the beginning, as at the end, God has primacy to operate in
Mary as in us "the will and the action."

IV. IS THERE A POINT WHERE
THE TWO CREST-LINES MEET?

The two lines leading along the crest issued from a positive
fact founded on the free choice of God. We have taken nothing
away, but always centered everything around these two lines of
thought, *Mater Dei,* and *Sponsa Verbi.* Is it possible to merge
these lines into a third, which would contain them? Or should
one of the two be given greater importance and receive the

---

48. The book by C. Dillenschneider quoted in L, II, p. 302 is one of
the most serious on this question.

other?[49] This work can only be done in *speculative theology,* for it belongs to a systematical order. Nevertheless we will give the essence of recent research.

It has been suggested that the two lines be joined by speaking of "sponsal maternity." This idea is expressed by the words *"brautliche Muttergottes"* (bridal Mother of God), a profound idea of Scheeben.[50] This notion is traditional, at least in its elements. But such as it is, does it go beyond a mere juxtaposition of words? It has recently been suggested to extend this idea of Scheeben. We have also used this idea as the central element in the second summit line of Mary, *Urbild der Kirche* (archetype of the Church), it would not merely be *one* aspect of Mariology (which is obvious), but *the principle* out of which *the entity* should be built; it would show the relationship of Mary with the Church as her *Urbild,* and not maternity, which should be the first among the ideas by which the privileges and the role of Mary are described, for at the center of the economy there is not Christ, the physical man, but the total Church.[51] This theory has great advantages, for example, in that it leaves the mediation of Christ intact, and this very clearly. But is it not faulty elsewhere in that it traces divine maternity, explicitly revealed in Scripture, back to the Church, *which is its consequence*? Is the distinction between the order of intention and execution a sufficient reason to answer this objection?[52] Should one take the theme of Mary, the New Eve as a point of departure in systematizing Mariology? It is certainly one element of the whole, but it cannot be its nucleus, for we can see in patristic tradition, if there is a relationship between Eve and Mary, the *New Eve* is rather the Church.[53]

---

49. C, I, p. 624 and L, II, p. 299.

50. C, I, p. 624.

51. C, I, p. 626.

52. L, II, pp. 299-300 and the thesis by A. Muller recorded in L, II, p. 297 (there is but "one maternity").

53. C, I, p. 625, n. 79.

It seems, therefore, that it is better to consider "sponsal maternity" and the idea of Mary as archetype and as the New Eve
as mere *elements* for speculation, and not to *focus* all the exposition on either of these ideas. We agree with Fr. Congar in that
there is another picture which embraces all three without showing
their disadvantages; it is of Mary, the *New Paradise*. Within the
bosom of Mariology itself, this picture manifests unity: through
the Immaculate Conception Mary is the New Paradise of God,
the new creation; through the Assumption Mary represents the
eschatological Paradise, anticipated in herself, by her divine and
virginal maternity, *which finds its central place here.* Mary appears
like the Paradise where God is received totally, where he finds
pleasure "in walking in the evening breeze," the closed garden
where the espousals of God and man take place in the incarnate
Christ.

The theological idea of Paradise indicates in itself the idea of
creature in as much as having become transparent to the divinity
which dwells in it, Mary, the New Paradise, clearly belongs in
the order *of creation.* Thus at the same time the danger of over-
shadowing Christ's mediation and co-redemption is avoided. As
the perfect creature, God's Paradise, Mary fulfills the perfect idea
of the creator, for she too is a co-operator in the grace of the
work of God.

This picture which we prefer because it maintains maternity
and sponsality on an equal level, without making the one subordinate to the other, is moreover patristic. It has a chance of
meeting with the sympathy of our Eastern brethren, and the
same time it is present in modern Marian treatises, for example,
in that of Grignion de Montfort.[54]

---

54. *Treatise on the True Devotion*, Par. 261, where the saint strikes a
traditional vein that was at that time forgotten in the West. On Marian
iconography, L, III, pp. 528-532.

CONCLUSION

Mariology has a role of gravitating around the central principles of theology; herein lies the secret of its balance as well as its wealth. In other words none of Mary's mysteries is opaque, there is none which screens the light from other mysteries, but on the contrary, all these mysteries are *transparent*, illuminated by other mysteries as they themselves illuminate others. Thus for example divine maternity moves around its center of gravity, *the incarnation of the divine Word*, for this is what gives account of both the free call and the free reply. The second crest line moves around the mystery of the Church; the Immaculate Conception moves around the Church according to its aspect as a return to the first Paradise; the Assumption around the Church in its aspect of the pilgrimage towards the eschatological Paradise.

It would therefore seem that, just as Mary was during her terrestrial life, so Marian mysteries are eclipsed by the light that comes from elsewhere, a light whose rays they reflect. As Marian mysteries seem to grow faint, they motion to us to pass on, not in order to forget them, but to penetrate more deeply by the light which fills them, into the mysteries of Christ, the Holy Spirit, and the Church and the end of all time.

We believe that this aspect of Mariology as a "theology of gravitation" has a chance of meeting the aspirations of our separated brethren. Above all we believe that we fulfill our intended purpose in this section, that is to show the place of Mariology in the *general religious* formation,

Nevertheless we know that these mysteries, which seem to be content with gravitating towards deeper mysteries, are their very source. Although everything comes from God's initiative in Jesus Christ, it is none the less true that without Mary the Word could not have been incarnate. Here is the unfathomable mystery of the love of God which recreates and respects its creature to the point that it needs Mary's *fiat* to cause the Incarnation. While Mary moves around the orbit of the Church, we know that she is the same time, previously, and from the chronological and onto-logical aspect, its transcendent archetype. In one word we know that the way in which Mariology seems to move around other mysteries hides the fact that Mary had uncommunicable and pre-eminent privileges, by her very person as Mother of God.

Mariology is in this way "the servant of theology" and explains it (besides Christology) from above. This paradox reveals in our opinion the Marian mystery already apparent in the Gospel whose seeming sobriety it explains, that is to say the self-effacement, the humility of the one who is the Mother of God. Just as we come up against the data of the Synoptics, whence we set out, we find again the twofold and unique mystery of salvation, that of grandeur veiled by humility. Mary cannot turn us away from Christ, for she realizes the inspired words, the soul of the work of Jesus; *Exinanivit semetipsum.*[55] (He spent Himself.)

---

55. We are becoming more acutely aware of considering the *first principle* of Mariology not as an axiom ... but as a source of light illuminating the person of the Mother of God in its different aspects. The "Study on Luke," I-II (R. Laurentin, *Structure et théologie de Luc,* Coll. Études bibliques), Paris, 1957 reopens discussion on two points. Had Mary from the beginning a perfect knowledge of her Son's divine character? Was her vow of virginity previous to, or was it influenced by, the grace of the Annunciation itself? Moreover the account given by Luke, who puts Mary in the place where the ancient law intersects the new, situates her entire testimony in a literary context steeped in a Pentecost faith. Research recalls the "existential" aspect of Mary. The survey of studies, which have appeared between 1955 and 1961, reveal an over-abundance of historical inquests by schools (made ever since Carolingian times) and reflections of bold speculation; on the other hand data on patristic and liturgic research is poor. While the connections between Mary and the Church, which have been closely examined in recent times, have accumulated the themes on mediation, co-redemption and Mary's royalty seem, even at the level of theological

schools, far from the desired clarity: their traditional basis does not seem
to worry the speculative theologians. The "piously and soberly" of the
First Vatican Council is more than ever necessary here. The best general
study is by G. Philips, *L'Orientation de la Mariologie contemporaine. Essai
bibliographique*, 1955-1959, in *Marianum* XXII (1960). Read also by the
same author: *Marie et l'Église*, in *Revue de clergé*, Sept. 1958, pp. 1-24,
(we have used this titled separately); *Beatae V. Mariae locus et munus in
Ecclesia*, in *Ephem. Mariologicae*, 1959, pp. 51-67; *Les fundements de la
Mariologie* in *Ephem. Mariologicae*, 1961, pp. 65-86. Mgr. G. Philips,
unites the concerns of traditional basis of Mariology with Schuern, *Le médi-
cin jusqu'au seuil du miracle* in *Maria et Ecclesia*, Vol. XIII, Rome, 1960
pp. 189-204 reminds us that the critical and scientific conditions of the
enquiries on Lourdes patients leaves much to be desired in precision.
(Note from 1962)